THE COMPLETE GUIDE TO TREEING WALKER COONHOUNDS

Ann Jayne

LP Media Inc. Publishing
Text copyright © 2021 by LP Media Inc.
All rights reserved.

www.lpmedia.org

Publication Data

Ann Jayne

The Complete Guide to Treeing Walker Coonhounds – First edition.

Summary: "Successfully raising a Treeing Walker Coonhound Dog from puppy to old age" – Provided by publisher.

ISBN: 978-1-954288-28-7

[1. Treeing Walker Coonhounds – Non-Fiction] I. Title.

Design by Sorin Rădulescu
First paperback edition, 2021

TABLE OF CONTENTS

CHAPTER 4

CHAPTER 5

For Casey and Bowie
Thank you for teaching me about your wonderful world.
I'm so thankful that God made dogs!

Welcome to the Wonderful World of Treeing Walker Coonhounds

Photo Courtesy of Ann Jayne

Bowie

I'm a dog lover. I always have been. I have a photograph of me when I was no more than two years old, sitting in a chair. I had on my little car coat and was holding one of my great-grandfather's beagle puppies. Pure, unfettered, absolute joy was emanating from the grin on my face and the sparkle in my eyes. That may be when my love for dogs, especially hounds, began.

I have had many dogs of various breeds. To date, I have had two Treeing Walker Coonhounds. Both of them were rescued. Casey was my first Treeing Walker Coonhound and through him, I fell in love with the Treeing Walker Coonhound breed. I learned so much about Treeing Walker Coonhounds from him. When Casey succumbed to cancer, I rescued Bowie, my second Treeing Walker Coonhound.

In no way do I consider myself an expert on dogs or dog behavior. No one knows everything about anything or everything. No. I'm not an expert trainer or behaviorist. But I am experienced. I have the deepest love for dogs that I think is possible. Until I meet my next dog. Then that love, which was thought to be at its zenith, grows even higher.

If you are a dog person, you know this. You don't need a book to tell you. The dog has already spoken those invisible words to you. Sealed them on your heart forever. Tattooed them on your very soul.

Perhaps you aren't a dog person. Not yet anyway. But you picked up this book to learn something. Something that might be missing from your life. And you want a dog to be a part of your life. Congratulations! You are about to embark on literally, a life-changing event by bringing a dog into your life. I promise you won't regret it. Oh, you might question your sanity sometimes. Who doesn't do that?

Photo Courtesy of Ann Jayne

Casey

But regrets? Never. One wag of the tail or a big old head with soft, floppy ears and large, soulful eyes that shoves itself under your hand is all it takes for everything to be forgiven.

Hopefully, this book motivates you to find that canine companion, or subsequent companions, who will become part of your life and whom you will never forget.

4

CHAPTER 1
A Brief History of the Treeing Walker Coonhound

Origins of the Treeing Walker Coonhound

The Treeing Walker Coonhound has been around since the mid-1700s. English Foxhounds that had been imported to America were bred with hounds in America to help establish Virginia Hounds. Thomas Walker, for

Photo Courtesy of Carly Ferguson

whom the Treeing Walker Coonhound is named, bred his Walker Foxhounds from these Virginia Hounds.

On November 20, 1852, a dog of unknown origin was stolen from a deer chase in Tennessee by Tom Harris. The dog, Tennessee Lead, was sold that very same day to George Washington Maupin and immediately bred to Red May, an English Walker Foxhound. Tennessee Lead was a big-boned, black and tan dog with tight hair. A photo of him looks like he might have been a precursor to, or descendant of, the Black and Tan Coonhound, which developed from crossing Bloodhounds to Virginia Foxhounds.

FUN FACT

National Treeing Walker Coonhound Association

The National Treeing Walker Coonhound Association (NTWCA) is the official American Kennel Club (AKC) Parent Club for the breed. The NTWCA is dedicated to the promotion and protection of the Treeing Walker Coonhound breed and currently operates as a private group on Facebook. For more information about this association, visit www.facebook.com/groups/NTWCAparentclub.

Tennessee Lead was noted for his drive and speed in chasing red foxes. He became a proficient stud, contributing to the Foxhound breed. George Washington, the George Washington, the first President of the United States of America, was a key player in developing the American Foxhound.

The Treeing Walker Coonhound developed through the years, with Tennessee Lead being bred to various other hounds from Kentucky, Georgia, Maryland, and England. By 1868, the Maupins had bred a distinctive hound. Breeding continued, but so did dismal record-keeping, until Maupin's nephew began keeping records of the breeding. His dog, Spotted Top, was descended from Tennessee Lead and native hounds. Spotted Top was bought by the Walker Brothers of Garrard County, Kentucky. His bloodlines began appearing throughout the South, including Missouri, Texas, and Tennessee.

Tennessee Lead was such a powerful influence in the Treeing Walker Coonhound breed that a historical marker was erected by the Tennessee Historical Commission. The marker is located north of Obey Park Road (on the left when traveling north) on Livingston Highway (SR111) in Monroe, Overton County, Tennessee. The inscription reads:

Near here in November, 1852, a black and tan hound was stolen out of a deer chase by a horse trader, taken to Madison County, Kentucky, sold to George Washington Maupin. There, as Tennessee Lead, he became the foundation sire of all Walker, Trigg, and Goodman fox hounds.

Although the Treeing Walker Coonhound was developing, it would not be recognized as a true distinct breed for nearly another century.

In 1945, the United Kennel Club (UKC) recognized the Treeing Walker Coonhound as a separate breed from foxhounds and other breeds of coonhounds. Although the Treeing Walker Coonhound has been eligible to compete in American Kennel Club (AKC) Companion Events since January 1, 2004, the breed was not admitted to the AKC until 2012! The Treeing Walker Coonhound became the 175th dog breed and 6th coonhound breed to be recognized by the AKC. The official AKC Parent Club for the Treeing Walker Coonhound is the National Treeing Walker Coonhound Association. AKC Breed Clubs and Rescue Networks are located throughout the United States, allowing you to connect with other Treeing Walker Coonhound lovers.

Along with the AKC and UKC, the Treeing Walker Coonhound is now recognized by the American Canine Association (ACA), American Canine Registry (ACR), American Pet Registry, Inc. (APRI), Continental Kennel Club (CKC), Dog Registry of America, Inc. (DRA), North American Purebred Registry, Inc. (NAPR), and the National Kennel Club (NKC).

Today's Treeing Walker Coonhound is a breed that is 100% Made in America! As the name implies, Treeing Walker Coonhounds were bred to tree raccoons. They take their job seriously and perform it with delight and gusto. Once a raccoon is treed, the hounds will bay until the owner catches up. These dogs run like rockets off leash and outrun their owners on the hunt in a matter of seconds. (Note that this speediness exists whether you hunt raccoons or not.) During a treeing session, the hounds will spend a considerable amount of time standing on their back legs, throwing their heads back to an almost unnatural position while barking and baying furiously. The hound will hold the raccoon at bay, jumping up and down on his/her hindlegs trying to get up the tree. Sometimes, with a nice running start, these marvelous hunters can jump upwards of five or six feet. If there are enough low branches or the tree is growing at an angle, Treeing Walker Coonhounds can actually *climb* trees while vigorously pursuing their quarry.

Raccoons are not the only animals that Treeing Walker Coonhounds will chase. Squirrels, rabbits, deer, and rats can be objects of interest and pursuit for these dogs as well. Bobcats, bears, and even mountain lions are not off limits, either. Even gophers in the ground aren't safe as these hounds, ever on the hunt, will be able to smell if the gopher is present or not. If the gopher is down below, the digging and woofing commence. If you happen to be behind a digging Treeing Walker Coonhound, move aside as dirt will fly back at an alarming speed.

*Photo Courtesy of
Erica Perez*

Physical Characteristics

Male Treeing Walker Coonhounds stand about 25-27 inches tall. Females are usually an inch or two shorter.

Treeing Walker Coonhounds are a sturdy breed, even though they may be very trim and appear to be fine-boned. They are also a hardy breed and, when on the hunt, can run all night. Treeing Walker Coonhounds are super sweet dogs with an excellent disposition.

Treeing Walker Coonhounds have short coats that are easily managed without extensive grooming or fancy cuts. So if you have a dog bathing area

Photo Courtesy of
Julia Bland

in your house, giving your Treeing Walker Coonhound a bath shouldn't be much of a problem. Keep in mind, though, that if you have to lift the dog into a tub, you will be lifting at least 60 pounds. But you will save hundreds of dollars a year by not having to get hair clipped, snipped, styled or brushed out. If you live in a warm climate, or it's summer, get the garden hose and some shampoo and let your coonhound have a bath al fresco.

However, Treeing Walker Coonhounds are shedders. Not big shedders, but enough. The hair is short, so while you won't be able to stuff a mattress or knit a sweater like you would with a Great Pyrenees or German Shepherd, there still will be dog hair around. On your couch. On your chair. On your black yoga pants as you leave the house to go teach a yoga class. Keep in mind that a little dog hair never hurt anyone.

Treeing Walker Coonhounds are more common in the southern United States, but they adapt readily to most climates, including the frigid northern states and even Alaska. So if you want to add a Treeing Walker Coonhound to your family, and you live somewhere that has harsh winters, you will need to get your Treeing Walker Coonhound a dog blanket and make sure he/she has warm shelter from the elements. A dog bed by the fire place or a couch works nicely.

There are two color varieties of the Treeing Walker Coonhounds. The first is tri-colored, consisting of black, brown and white. Hounds may be a definite, and obvious, tri-color with a black saddle and brown and white legs. The head is normally brown and might have a white blaze or stripe. Brown ticking is present on their legs. Another variation, while still considered tri-color, is for the dog to be white with large black and/or brown spots, ticking on the legs and a brown head. The second color variety is bi-color, mostly black and white with very little brown coloring.

Regardless of their colorations, Treeing Walker Coonhounds are strikingly beautiful dogs. Sometimes the spots on their coat look like shapes. Bowie, my second rescued Treeing Walker Coonhound, has large black spots on his belly. It looks like someone stamped his belly with black dots. Bowie also has a perfect black heart on his right side by his hip and thigh and a pair of black angel wings on his left side. I consider these special spots gifts from God and Casey. Casey had a small white heart on his black saddle.

Treeing Walker Coonhounds usually weigh around 50-70 pounds. Active hunting dogs are very trim and will be on the lighter weight side. Many pets, although they may be fairly active, may be in the middle or north end of the recommended weight. Some Treeing Walker Coonhounds might easily accelerate to a few pounds north of 70 pounds, so their diet, including treats, will need to be monitored.

Disposition

Even though they are all business while hunting, Treeing Walker Coonhounds have a wonderful and sweet disposition. They make an excellent pet, are extremely affectionate, and docile with children. When you bring a Treeing Walker Coonhound into your family, you aren't just getting

Photo Courtesy of Wendi Sopkin

a dog. You are acquiring a new member of your family. They can be equally comfortable at home on the couch or in your lap as they are in the woods. These dogs are incredibly smart and might easily outfox their owner or canine siblings if there is something they want. More on that later...

For a semi-large dog, Treeing Walker Coonhounds are relatively long-lived with an average life span of 13 years. Some live to be older than that. These dogs definitely know how to make the most of their life, whether it is running in the woods, running in the yard, or running to the couch.

AKA

Treeing Walker Coonhounds are part of an entire coonhound family. Besides Treeing Walkers, there are Bluetick Coonhounds, Redtick Coonhounds (English Coonhound), Redbone Coonhounds, and Black and Tan Coonhounds. Plott Hounds, Fox Hounds and Black Mouth Curs can also be labeled as coonhounds because of their treeing and hunting abilities as well as their appearance.

Coonhound dogs are affectionately referred to as "coonies" or maybe just "coonhound." Sometimes, Treeing Walker Coonhounds are referred to as "Walker Hounds" as well.

Be prepared for innocent passersby to say something like, "That's a tall beagle!"

As the mother of a beagle and a Treeing Walker Coonhound, I have encountered this on numerous walks, trips to the vet, or to the store.

"Your beagles are sure cute!"

I thank people and then educate them. Many of them have never heard of a Treeing Walker Coonhound. I've seen collars and bandanas that say "I'm not a beagle!"

"They sure look like beagles."

Yes they do.

CHAPTER 2

Preparing for Your Treeing Walker Coonhound

Before you bring your new family member home, you will need to ensure that you have the supplies you need and that your house and yard are ready to accommodate your new Treeing Walker Coonhound. Hint: you'll discover that you forgot something or need 15 more things. Just get ready for that.

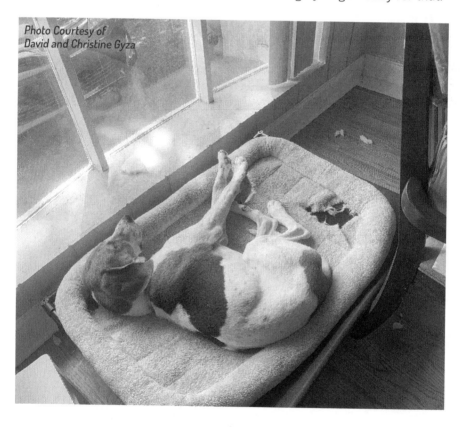

Photo Courtesy of David and Christine Gyza

Securing Your Yard

Owning any kind of dog can be expensive. While bringing a Treeing Walker Coonhound into your life and house doesn't necessarily require an extensive remodel, the first thing you should determine is if you have an adequately fenced yard. A six- or eight-foot stockade fence or iron/metal bar fence should be sufficient; however, keep in mind that your new buddy might be able to easily scale the fence

FUN FACT
How Popular Are They?

According to the AKC, the Treeing Walker Coonhound breed was ranked 137th most popular out of 197 breeds in 2020. The AKC determines breed popularity based on the number of dogs registered with their organization from each breed annually. TWCs were ranked 129th in 2019 and 137th in 2018.

and escape. Coonhounds can climb, remember? Also, if you have a metal bar fence, ensure that the poles/bars are not spaced far enough apart for a coonhound to get his head stuck in between the poles or bars.

Walk around your yard and check for holes around your fence. Pretend you are a cowboy out checking the fence to make sure the herd doesn't get away.

When we got Ajax, our beagle, as a puppy, we did this very thing. We had a large pie-shaped yard with a stockade fence. There were a few places with beagle puppy-sized holes so we put rocks in the holes. We also got metal garden edging and hammered it down along the bottom of the fence.

If your fence is an older stockade fence there may be some rotted places near the bottom. Or critters may have dug under it. If it is chain link, make sure the bottom of the chain link is secured and not curling up, providing an escape route for a puppy. Believe me, they will find it! And even if there is a hole in the middle of your stockade fence, chances are pretty high that at some point, your Treeing Walker Coonhound will notice it. He might see something through the hole that needs to be chased. Patch the small hole now so you don't have to chase down your coonhound and patch a larger hole later.

Check the gates, too. If they are loose, get new hinges. If they have a flip latch, put a carabiner in the hole of the latch to keep it from opening. Canine snouts can easily push up a flip latch. It might take some work, or it might not. Most stockade fence gates have latches that, over time, slip and are easily pushed open, say by a beagle named Ajax who thinks he and his old beagle brother Rascal need a night on the town at midnight in January. Yeah. Get that carabiner first thing!

We moved to our current house four years ago and thought that our metal bar fence would be sufficient for Ajax and our little rescue beagle Lucy. Lucy was a tiny little lemon and white beagle and frightened of everything. The first thing she did was squeeze through the bars and run away! Luckily our neighbor saw her and told us. So, my husband, David, and I went to the hardware store and bought a roll of green, PVC-coated, steel mesh chicken wire fence. It was 6-feet high so we cut it in half and zip-tied it around the lower portion of our nice, metal bar fence, as well as the gates. It looked super-attractive. But it worked. Little Lucy wasn't able to escape again.

This type of mesh chicken wire can be pulled away and bent, however. Casey, my first rescued Treeing Walker Coonhound, protected the yard as *his* yard. Maintenance men who happened to be working nearby were seen as a threat and Casey barked and pulled and clawed at the mesh chicken wire fence, pulling it back and smashing it down. It was sad-looking but easily zip-tied back to the metal bars, enhancing the curb appeal of our fence. Bowie has now pulled off the mesh chicken wire on the north side of the yard while he chases squirrels or deer. The mesh chicken wire is pretty well ruined so we will need to replace it.

I know some people who have put chicken wire fencing (the small chicken wire for actual chickens) down, perpendicular to the bottom of their fence (on the grass, for non-math people like me), to prevent their dogs from digging out. If your coonhound turns out to be a digger, this might be another option for you. The grass will grow over it so it won't be as noticeable as say, green steel mesh chicken wire on a black metal bar fence.

Another option for fencing is invisible fencing. While I have never used this type of fencing, friends on my "Life With My Rescued Coonhound" Facebook group have. For most of the coonhound owners, after their dogs were trained, the invisible fence works very well. For a few others, it did not. Their coonhounds seemed to prefer a shock in order to pursue game. The electric fence will not keep out other dogs or wildlife, so that, and a power outage, are things to consider.

If you happen to have a swimming pool, you might install a fence around it. Some cities require this. Having owned two Treeing Walker Coonhounds, I have discovered that neither Casey nor Bowie were ever interested in the pool. But, it may be a good idea to let your coonhound know where the steps are just in case he ever falls into the pool so he will be able to get out.

Once you are comfortable that your yard is secure and Treeing Walker Coonhound escape-proof, it is time to do a safety inventory of your house and make any needed adjustments.

Preparing Your House

Regardless of whether you get a puppy, young pup, or older Treeing Walker Coonhound, you need to ensure that your house is ready for your new family member. Basically, it's like child-proofing your home for a toddler, except kids aren't too prone to chewing up things. At least my two boys didn't...

Treeing Walker Coonhound puppies aren't tiny like beagle puppies. They are taller and leggier and if you get a puppy that is old enough to leave its mother, it may be almost as tall as a beagle already.

When we got Ajax as a puppy, he loved to crawl under the couch or coffee table and bark at us. Pretty soon he got too big. If your furniture is close to the floor, this probably won't be an issue for you with a Treeing Walker Coonhound puppy. But don't rule anything out.

However, with a puppy in the house, if you have fringe on the bottom of your couch or chairs, you will need to change that or you probably won't be happy about your Treeing Walker Coonhound's reaction to the fringe.

Photo Courtesy of
Emily Vacek

The same thing goes with rugs, whether they are antique Persian rugs or a throw rug from a discount store. Your puppy won't know the difference but I guarantee you, the Persian rug will taste much, much better and be much more fun to play with and chew on than the cheap rug. So until the house-breaking and chewing phase is over, it might be best to pack up the expensive rug for a while.

This is a good time to introduce chew toys. If you catch your puppy chewing on your rug or furniture, remove the puppy and hand it a toy, instilling in it that the toy is perfectly fine to chew on; the furniture and rugs are not. If you kick your shoes off when you flop down into your chair, remember that shoes will be fair game, too. Perhaps, they are even better because they smell like you. Put your shoes in your closet and close the door.

Puppy-proofing your house, or even proofing it for a teenager or mature dog, means you might have to crawl around at Treeing Walker Coonhound height and see what the dog might see. Or what the tail might find when wagging furiously. All expensive and breakable items should be placed on a high shelf or even in another room.

With regard to your floors, Treeing Walker Coonhounds usually have no problem walking or running on tile, carpet, vinyl, or hardwood floors. Your hardwood floors might get a little distressed, but can easily be sanded at some point.

While you are crawling around coonhound-proofing your house, check the electrical outlets and cords. A puppy will be curious and might decide the outlet needs a good sniffing with a wet nose and maybe a lick or two. Cords might need to be chewed on as well. Prevention is better. Put plugs in the outlets. Cover the cords or hide them as best as you can.

Case in point: when we got our beagle, Rascal, my husband and I were outside putting up a trampoline for our boys. We had a radio plugged in. All of a sudden we heard a POP! and BZZZT! followed by a sharp yelp from Rascal. It seems Rascal, for some unknown reason, had decided to investigate and subsequently lick or chew on the plugged-in cord. It didn't kill him, but it smarted. And a few minutes later he was back, sniffing around and getting ready for a big old lick until we yelled at him. So, never rule out anything. Ever.

Basically, be on the safe side. If there's something you think might get chewed on, move it. Your new Treeing Walker Coonhound will be curious about her new home and will want to explore it. That's okay, but make sure that Great-Grandma Gertrude's 200-year-old quilt isn't on the couch or chair. Put it in the closet.

An ounce of prevention is worth a pound of cure. Channel your inner Benjamin Franklin.

Toxic Plants

Many plants that are inside your house or in your yard can be toxic to your Treeing Walker Coonhound. Many of them might have healing qualities or provide delicious fruit, such as aloe vera and apple trees. But, these plants can be harmful when ingested!

The Animal Poison Control Center (APCC) Hotline is 1-888-426-4435. It is open 24 hours, seven days/week. Keep this number on your refrigerator, posted somewhere outside (on your patio, perhaps) and in your cell phone contacts. Highlight this paragraph and dog ear the page.

If your coonhound does indeed ingest something, gather a sample of it. Contact the APCC and also your veterinarian. You should be able to text a photo of the plant that your dog ate. Wait for instructions from your veterinarian or someone at the APCC before you induce vomiting. It may cause more harm than good.

Many plants contain saponins, which can cause vomiting and diarrhea when ingested. Aloe Vera, relatively harmless as a topical gel, contains saponins which can be toxic for dogs. American Holly, English Ivy, and Hosta also have saponins and in addition to vomiting and diarrhea, hounds can experience abdominal pain, bloating, and excessive salivation.

Other plants which can cause distress, such as salivating, abdominal pain, vomiting and diarrhea are Amaryllis and Azaleas (eating the leaves can even be fatal). Hounds who ingest Cyclamen may experience seizures and die. The innocent-looking Daisy contains sesquiterpene, which can lead to uncoordinated movement in addition to salivating, vomiting and diarrhea. Kalanchoe can also cause abnormal heart rhythm. Along with vomiting and diarrhea, Mistletoe can also cause drooling, ataxia, seizures, and death. Morning Glories, consumed in large amounts, can cause agitation and incoordination, as well as vomiting and diarrhea. The roots of the Begonia contain calcium oxalates, which can cause vomiting and diarrhea.

Certain Lily plants are extremely poisonous to dogs. The Calla Lily contains calcium oxalates which can cause irritation, drooling, and difficulty swallowing in addition to vomiting and diarrhea. Some lilies, such as the Peace Lily and Peruvian Lily, may cause drooling and mouth irritation. The Tiger Lily, Day Lily, Asiatic Lily and the Easter Lily, can cause liver failure and be deadly.

Some bulb plants have high degrees of toxicity for our canine friends. The Autumn Crocus is more toxic than the Spring Crocus, causing a burning sensation in the mouth or possible seizures and/or liver damage. The Spring Crocus can upset the gastrointestinal tract, causing vomiting and diarrhea as well as drooling. While all parts of Daffodils and Tulips are poisonous, the bulbs are especially poisonous, causing vomiting, diarrhea, abdominal pain, seizures, and a drop in blood pressure. Iris can be a skin and stomach irritant, or cause vomiting, diarrhea, drooling, and lethargy.

Bark, branches, leaves, needles, stems, berries, and seeds of Juniper and Locust are poisonous. They can cause vomiting and diarrhea. The Locust can cause bloody diarrhea, difficulty breathing, and death.

As with daffodils and tulips, sometimes, the entire plant, every last part of it, can be poisonous. Such is the case with Foxglove and Wisteria. Digoxin and digitalis are cardiac glycosides found in Foxglove. Under controlled use and prescriptions, they help people with heart failure or abnormal rhythms. Ingestion of the plant or its roots directly can cause an irregular heartbeat or slow down the heart rate.   The flowers and seeds of the Wisteria plant are the most dangerous to dogs, even though the whole plant is toxic. Ingestion of the seeds and flowers can cause dogs to be confused, dizzy, nauseous, have stomach pains, diarrhea, vomit repeatedly, collapse, or even die.

Cardiac glycosides are also found in Oleander. A dog who ingests Oleander may experience irregularities in heart function, muscle tremors, vomiting and diarrhea.

Fleabane, which can keep away fleas and grows all over the United States, is mildly toxic. It can cause indigestion and an upset stomach. Dieffenbachia, a popular houseplant, can cause swelling in the mouth and throat, stinging in the mouth, and excessive drooling.

Cyanogenic glucosides, found in plants like the Hydrangea, can cause lethargy, depression, vomiting, diarrhea, increased heart rate, and increased body temperature.

Pacific Yew leaves that are ingested can cause tremors, respiratory distress, heart failure, seizures, vomiting, and death. The Sago Palm is one of the deadliest plants if ingested by dogs. It can cause bleeding disorders, liver failure, and death.

Marijuana should never be given to dogs. The tetrahydrocannabinol (THC) can cause depression, incoordination, excessive salivation, dilated pupils, and possibly put your hound in a coma. Dogs can tolerate CBD Oil, which is different from THC.

All of the plants in the Crassulaceae family, including the Jade Plant, are poisonous to dogs. Convulsions, slower heart rate, vomiting, abdominal pain, weakness, lethargy and depression can occur if the dog ingests these plants.

There are also some "people food" plants that, in some forms, can be toxic to dogs.

- **APPLE TREE**: While apples are not poisonous to dogs, the leaves, stems and seeds contain cyanide. Wilted leaves dropped in the fall can cause panting, dilated pupils, and difficulty breathing.
- **BAY LAUREL**: Although it is excellent for seasoning, eugenol is a component that can cause excessive salivation, vomiting, and even kidney failure in your hound.
- **CHERRY TREE**: The leaves and branches contain cyanogenic glycosides and cherry pits contain cyanide, leading to difficulty in breathing, dilated pupils, and going into shock.
- **GARLIC:** Can cause anemia through a breakdown of red blood cells, affect the heart rate, cause general weakness, or can be poisonous.
- **GRAPES**: The toxicity varies from dog to dog and by the amount consumed. Liver failure and kidney failure can occur. This goes for raisins and currants, as well.
- **HOPS**: Can cause panting and increased body temperature, which can lead to seizures and death. The yeast is also bad for your dog. No beer for your coonhound!
- **NICOTIANA,** basically nicotine, is bad for humans and dogs. It can cause your dog to become hyperactive, soon to be followed by depression, vomiting, incoordination, paralysis and death. Don't hand your dog a cigarette to smoke while drinking his beer.
- **TOMATO PLANT** stems and leaves are toxic to dogs. Ingestion of these can cause your dog's heart rate to slow down, cause excessive salivation, depression, dilated pupils and a severely upset stomach. Tomatoes themselves, including tomato sauce (in case your Treeing Walker Coonhound gets a bite of pizza or spaghetti), are not harmful at all to your dog.

So, while you are hound-proofing your house and yard, notice if you have any of these plants around. If you have any house plants sitting in your window sills, that are within easy reach of a Treeing Walker Coonhound, especially a puppy, move them to a higher place. Even if the plants aren't harmful, move them to a higher location just in case your hound decides to attack the plants for no other reason than it is extremely fun.

Toxic Household Chemicals and Medications

More than 200,000 dogs are accidentally poisoned each year from household products. Along with toxic plants, ensure that all hazardous chemicals and medications, including healthy supplements, are placed out of reach of a Treeing Walker Coonhound. And by out of reach, I mean really out of reach! Treeing Walker Coonhounds can be taller than four feet when they are standing on their hind legs. Simply moving something to the back of the counter may not be an obstacle for your coonhound because he can s-t-r-e-t-c-h. Dangerous, or potentially dangerous, items need to be placed on the top shelf or in an extremely secure area. Bathroom and laundry room doors should be kept closed to keep your hound out of that area. However, most kitchens are relatively open, so you might consider keeping a childproof lock on your kitchen sink cabinet doors in case your coonhound decides to see what is under the sink. If you are unfortunate enough to have a mouse in your house, your coonhound might pursue it, even if the mouse squeezes through the kitchen sink cabinet door.

Coonhounds can paw at a cabinet door until it opens. They can pull on, or paw at, the knobs or handles, too. Although dishwasher detergent or steel wool pads might not taste good after the first bite, they could still cause harm even after a brief ingestion. Luckily, Casey never bothered with the kitchen sink cabinet doors. To date, Bowie hasn't either. But it is a good idea to keep an eye out on your Treeing Walker Coonhound when he is in the kitchen, just in case.

Keep the following dog toxins out of your Treeing Walker Coonhound's reach:

- All medications (prescription and over-the-counter) and supplements, including Tylenol. They can cause vomiting, diarrhea, anemia. Sometimes, just ingesting one pill can cause serious health issues.

- Dog medications, including flea and tick products (avoid products with Tetrachlorvinphos and Dichlorvos), especially if they taste really good! Too much application of topical medications, such as flea control products, can cause severe itching or interfere with the nervous system, causing seizures, tremors and excessive drooling.

- All household cleaners, particularly those that contain bleach, ammonia, and phosphates can cause pale gums, internal bleeding, bloody feces and urine, nosebleeds, excessive thirst, excessive drooling, heavy breathing, and muscle tremors. Toilet bowl cleaners, automatically added when flushing, or residual amounts from cleaning, can harm your dog. Don't let your dog ever drink from your toilet and keep the lid down on your toilet.

- Rodenticides cause bruising, nosebleeds, sore joints, bloody vomit and feces.

- Insecticides can cause the same symptoms as household cleaners, including lethargy.

- Slug and snail poisons contain sugar and metaldehyde which tastes good to dogs but can cause blindness, excessive salivation, seizures and death.

- Anti-freeze (ethylene glycol) smells and tastes sweet to dogs. It is one of the most dangerous things your dog can ingest. Anti-freeze causes seizures, staggering, depression, increased water consumption, increase in urination with a decrease in urine output, and vomiting. Get your coonhound to the veterinarian as fast as possible.

- Essential oils: cinnamon, citrus, pennyroyal, peppermint, pine, sweet birch, tea tree, wintergreen and ylang can cause burns or irritation whether they are applied directly or diffused. Diffusing these oils can make the coonhound feel sick and if they are stuck in the house, there is no way for them to get some fresh air. Remember that your precious Treeing Walker Coonhound is a scent hound, so the smells, vapors and aromas might be especially strong and irritating for her.

- Moth balls containing naphthalene cause vomiting, diarrhea, anemia, weakness and collapsing. Paradichlorobenzene in moth balls can cause liver damage, seizures and staggering.

- Products for your yard, such as fertilizer and weed killer, that include orthophosphates and carbamates, can increase the risk for bladder cancer, cause aggression, tremors, seizures, weight loss and vomiting.

- Lead, included in old paint, flooring, or furniture as well as construction dust or fishing weights, causes vomiting, diarrhea, and anemia.

- Zinc, found in pennies (after 1982), hardware including nuts and bolts, fishing weights, nails, shampoos, cosmetics, and paint can cause anemia, vomiting, diarrhea, red or orange urine, and a lack of appetite.

- Artificial fragrances in your personal hygiene products (cosmetics, hair and skin care products, deodorant, soaps and gels), essential oils, laundry detergent, air fresheners, dryer sheets, fabric softeners, candles, and other cleaning products can cause a multitude of issues. Endocrine disruption, fatigue, dizziness, irritation of the gut, respiratory problems, kidney damage or problems in the central nervous system can occur. These artificial fragrances can mimic the dog's hormones, causing cancer, birth defects, developmental disorders, immune disorders and nerve damage.

Supplies and Toys

Getting ready for your Treeing Walker Coonhound is like preparing for the arrival of a baby (if you have kids). Some basic items needed will be:

- **A DOG BED.** This can quickly escalate to a dog bed in every room. We have six. Yes, six. Two in the living room, two in the study room (Bowie and Ajax lay in them and help me write, so I need to count them as references), and two in my bedroom. A full-grown Treeing Walker Coonhound will need a larger bed. They like to stretch out. They will also curl up in a small bed, perfecting the "coonie curl." Casey liked laying in the tiny dog bed we had for Lucy in our closet.

- **TOYS.** Treeing Walker Coonhounds love a variety of toys, from hard plastic toys to fuzzy animals with squeakers. The squeakers may be promptly extracted by the coonhound as he makes his "kill." Throw away the squeakers to prevent a trip to the veterinary emergency room because the dog won't swallow the squeaker during normal business hours. Fuzzy toys, especially fuzzy toys that crinkle to mimic the attack and "killing" of said toy, are also loads of fun. They are the most fun when you are watching a sad or dramatic movie. There are also toys made out of Kevlar and other tough-as-nails material. These are a good investment.

If your coonhound enjoys excursions with you, take him to the store (if dogs are allowed), and let him pick out his own toys! Plastic bones or deer antlers are a great way for your Treeing Walker Coonhound to chew to his heart's content. However, keep track of these toys as they are chewed on and whittled away. You don't want them getting too small so they can be easily swallowed or stuck in your coonhound's mouth. That's a trip to the ER just waiting to happen.

Make sure that your coonhound's other toys are large enough to not get swallowed. Small toys are okay for a small puppy, but not a larger dog. Everyone has single socks since they magically disappear in the dryer. Stuff one sock with four or five other socks, tie a knot in the sock, and you have an instant, cheap toy that smells like you. For an added bonus, stick a treat in one of the socks and your Treeing Walker Coonhound will spend some time dismantling the sock to get the treat!

Old throw pillows are fun if you like to pick up stuffing. Let your coonhound know that old pillows are okay, but if he grabs a good one, make an obnoxious sound, like a buzzer, (more on the word "NO!" later) and take the pillow away, putting it where it is safe.

- A large and sturdy crate if you are going to crate-train your Treeing Walker Coonhound. I'll talk more about this later.

- Blankets are always appreciated. Get your Treeing Walker Coonhound her very own (washable) blanket. Grab a cheap one at a thrift store or discount store. While you're at it, get a pretty blanket to throw over the couch to keep off some of the dog hair. If you have a particularly favorite blanket or one that you cherish, put it away. I guarantee you it will become your Treeing Walker Coonhound's favorite blanket, too. Old blankets and rugs are great to put in doghouses outside, too. While they provide warmth and comfort, they also look good laying around on the patio or in the yard because your coonhound will drag anything in the doghouse out of the doghouse.

- Food and water bowls. Metal bowls for food and water are easy to clean. For outdoors, especially if you have more than one dog, get a five- or eight-gallon bucket and keep it full of fresh, clean water. It will need to be cleaned occasionally as algae builds up in it. Have a bowl for water for your Treeing Walker Coonhound inside as well. I keep Bowie's in the kitchen by the back door on the tile floor. Coonhounds slurp and splash. Refilling the bowl can cause spills as well as the slurping and splashing. Don't put the water bowl on your expensive Persian rug. Avoid putting

Photo Courtesy of
Greg Amstone

the water bowl on a cute dog mat because over time the spilled water can cause the mat to get moldy. I learned this the hard way.

- Leashes, collars, identification tags and harnesses. Collars and leashes come in as many colors, materials, and varieties that you can imagine. Plain and simple leather or nylon collars are fine. Maybe you want to go a little crazy with style (and your wallet) and get a beaded or bejeweled collar. Knock yourself out. Whichever collar you decide on, get your dog some "jewelry," namely a pet ID with the name of your Treeing Walker Coonhound on it as well as your name and phone number.

Harnesses with leashes are a good option for walks rather than single leashes. A harness with a leash is better if your coonhound pulls. You can also get a pronged collar, plastic or metal, to help train your coonhound not to pull on you or the leash. This collar should only be used on walks. If you are raising and training a Treeing Walker Coonhound Puppy, pulling on the leash may never be an issue. It may or may not be an issue with an older or more exuberant dog. Many times, the teenage coonhound or even an older hound, may just be really excited about going for a walk, so that could be the only time they pull. Once they are into the walk for a while, the pulling may stop. So a pronged collar may only be needed for a little while. A professional trainer can also be very useful in teaching your Treeing Walker Coonhound not to pull on you as well as staying in his place, "heeling," so she won't chase other animals.

Expenses

In 2019, Americans spent nearly $96 billion (billion with a "b") on their pets. Of the $96 billion with a "b", nearly $37 billion of it was spent on pet food while $30 billion was spent on veterinary care. Factor in pet health insurance, boarding, doggy day care, grooming, monthly gift box subscriptions for your pet, birthday parties (yes, birthday parties) and pet pedicures, and $96 billion will be hit in no time.

As noted in Chapter 1, your grooming expenses will be minimal, perhaps just the cost of water and shampoo if you bathe your coonhound at home. Treeing Walker Coonhounds don't need a bath every week. In fact, they can go a few months at a time without getting a bath, unless they roll in poop or something dead (note that that is super fun!). They just aren't really smelly dogs. And, as was noted, there won't be a need for any fancy hair cutting. Wash. Dry. Done.

Kristen, my groomer, charges $30.00 each to bathe and dry Bowie and Ajax. The 20 bucks also includes filing their nails with a dog Dremel, cleaning their ears, and expressing their anal glands. Bowie and Ajax also get sprayed with "manly" spray so they smell great for several days! I call that a bargain. So I spend $50.00 (I tip her for each dog) about every three months. Actually, it costs me a little more than $50.00 as I get Kristen donut holes, too. And I can't drive through the donut shop without getting a pig-in-a-blanket for Bowie and donut holes for Ajax, as well as a pig-in-a-blanket for Kristen's whippet, Patches. Patches expects it from me when I come in and goes to his bed so I can tear up the said delectable for his dining pleasure.

Pet insurance may or may not be a good investment. I know people who swear by it and others who say it is a waste of money. Check with your veterinarian and see what they recommend. Check around for the best premiums and reimbursements. There may be age limit restrictions. If you adopt a 10-year-old Treeing Walker Coonhound, it may be extremely expensive, or impossible, to get pet health insurance for him.

I did a quick search for pet insurance. Keep in mind that I'm not a math or numbers gal. My eyes kind of began to glaze over while doing this brief research. But I persevered just for you!

- The lowest premium I found for dogs is $20.00/month ($240.00/year). You will need to check and see if the policy covers multiple dogs or if you need a policy for each dog.
- Deductibles range from $100 to $1000.
- Reimbursements vary from 60-90%.
- Hereditary issues may be covered, but there could be a waiting period of up to one year.
- Many policies won't insure a dog over the age of 10 years.
- Many policies will not cover pre-existing conditions.
- Benefits may be capped.
- Policies may or may not cover dental procedures.
- Some companies will make their software available to veterinarians so your vet can file the claim.
- Some policies may offer a "shrinking deductible" that reduces your deductible each year that you don't file a claim. So if your Treeing Walker Coonhound remains healthy, your deductible might actually decrease.

On average, for normal dog-owning Americans, $1000 is about what your Treeing Walker Coonhound will cost you per year. Obviously, if there are no health issues or surgeries/injuries, your expenses will be even less. No one can foresee a health crisis or injury for their Treeing Walker Coonhound. Please don't let that deter you from getting your hound. Budget for your dog and enjoy him or her.

CHAPTER 3

Adopting/Rescuing Your Treeing Walker Coonhound

This chapter is near and dear to my heart. In 2017, I found Casey, my first Treeing Walker Coonhound, starving on the street. I texted my husband and told him I was bringing a starving dog home. That was that. I fell in love with this dog, naming him after my great-grandfather, Franklin Martin Casey, on the drive home. It didn't take me long to fall in love with the Treeing Walker Coonhound breed, either.

I grew up in Okemah, Oklahoma. In 2015, the Animal Rescue League of Okemah (ARLO) was founded. For several weeks before Casey and I rescued each other, he had been wandering the streets of Okemah. He was skin and bones with a rope or chain burn on his neck and a gash on his right side. ARLO had tried and tried, unsuccessfully, to get him. He wouldn't come up to anyone. One woman left food out for him and after I brought him back to Edmond, she noticed that he wasn't around and put out an alert to ARLO and on Facebook. One of the Facebook members told me that I was "the only one he stuck to." My heart melted.

FUN FACT
Who Was Thomas Walker?

Thomas Walker was an explorer and physician who lived in Virginia in the 18th century. It's believed that Walker brought Walker Foxhounds to America in 1742, an action that laid the groundwork for the TWC breed. A Walker Foxhound was later crossed with a dog of unknown origin named Tennessee Lead, which resulted in what we now know as the Treeing Walker Coonhound.

Casey had a wonderful life while I was blessed to be his mom. When I found him, he weighed 42 pounds. Treeing Walker Coonhounds are supposed to weigh at least 60 pounds. My family fell in love with him and he fell in love with them.

Photo Courtesy of Julia Bland

I had Casey for 2 years, 3 months, and 19 days before he went to heaven from complications from spinal cancer. During that brief time, I learned so much about Treeing Walker Coonhounds. I am continuing to learn, having adopted Bowie only a few days after Casey died.

Bowie was in an ARLO foster home with another Treeing Walker Coonhound, Bella, who had been left at the animal shelter. Her family decided she wasn't worth saving. Bowie came to ARLO when a friend heard him yelping and crying, locked up in a shed in the woods. Bowie had been chewed up, possibly used as a bait dog for fighting dogs, and had been shot with buck shot. He was left to die.

Strongly Consider Adoption

Until I found Casey, I had no idea about the abuse, torment, and cruelty that plague many coonhounds. I highly recommend adopting one of these dogs.

Treeing Walker Coonhounds, as well as other coonhound breeds, are more common in the southern and southeastern areas of the United States. They are popular during hunting season, and then, many are discarded, dumped, abandoned, or starved. While many owners take excellent care of their coonhounds, there are many who do not. Animal shelters throughout the south will be bursting at the seams with coonhounds when hunting season ends.

Besides Treeing Walker Coonhounds, other purebred dogs can be found at animal shelters. In fact, purebred dogs might possibly make up the majority of dogs in animal shelters. In California alone, chihuahuas make up 30% of the dogs in shelters! The 12 breeds that are found in animals shelters the most are:

- American Bulldog
- Australian Cattle Dog
- Beagle
- Border Collie
- Boxer
- Chihuahua
- Dachshund
- German Shepherd
- Jack Russell Terrier
- Labrador Retriever
- Pit Bulls
- Rottweilers

Why? Well, for one thing, people don't do their research. If they did, they would know that German Shepherds and Border Collies need to be challenged because they are so intelligent, or that beagles "bark too much," or Rottweilers "get too big." Jack Russells tend to be hyperactive and Pit Bulls are way overbred.

*Photo Courtesy of
Kyle & Brook Underwood*

You are researching Treeing Walker Coonhounds and will know what to expect of this breed because you are reading this book. Perhaps after reading this, you decide that a Treeing Walker Coonhound isn't the dog for you. I hope that is not the case, but it is so much better to find out now than later.

Decide What Age is Best For You

Although I think that any age of a Treeing Walker Coonhound is suitable for anyone's lifestyle, you will need to make that decision. A puppy (or puppies) will occupy a considerable amount of your time. Casey was about six years old when I rescued him. Bowie was around four years old.

Older dogs, especially dogs who have been kept outside and/or had little socialization, may need house-training and obedience training. If you are looking for a dog to go on walks or jogs with, adopt a Treeing Walker Coonhound that is at least six to eight months old. Your new dog will relish exercising with you!

If you aren't too picky about what age of dog you want to get, and maybe your heart isn't necessarily set on a puppy, then your options with a rescue will greatly increase. Never rule out a senior dog, either. These dogs have been around the block twice but they still have so much love to give. More often than not, they just want a loving hand, tender voice, soft bed and full belly for the rest of their days. If you're not active, a senior dog may be your best choice. And best friend.

Finding a Rescue Organization

Once you have decided on the age of Treeing Walker Coonhound that you want to adopt, what do you do now?

First of all, check with your local rescues and animal shelters. Chances are, animal shelters in big cities will have a coonhound or two. Perhaps small-town shelters and rescues will, too. Many rescues network with each other so even if the rescue that you support doesn't have a Treeing Walker Coonhound, they should be able to find one for you fairly quickly.

Most people who work for an animal rescue organization are volunteers and may not be able to look for a coonhound for you right now. It may take them a few days, but they will look. You can do some research yourself and check the internet for Treeing Walker Coonhound rescues, or coonhound rescues in general that aren't specific for Treeing Walker

31

Coonhounds, but will probably have one. Even breed-specific coonhound rescues might have a Treeing Walker Coonhound, so check them out. Breed-specific rescues for just about any breed of dog you might be trying to find exist, too.

If you find a Treeing Walker Coonhound but it is in another state, don't let that deter you. Many rescues will transport the dog to you!

The rescue organizations should have photos of the dogs as well as a brief description, including the approximate age of the coonhound, disposition, health and any treatments for which the hound is being treated or has been treated.

Get Pre-Approved For Adoption

Pre-approval for adoption will be required if there currently isn't a Treeing Walker Coonhound available. However, getting pre-approved will move you to the top of the list should a coonhound become available.

If the rescue takes all breeds and mixed breeds of dogs, it could take a while to get a Treeing Walker Coonhound as rescues never know what they will get on any given day. So if the wait is going to be too long, you might also get pre-approved with a coonhound rescue organization. The chances of them having, and getting, a Treeing Walker Coonhound should be higher, and that could reduce the waiting time for you to get your coonhound.

Once you are pre-approved, let the rescue organization keep your application active. You may decide that you want another Treeing Walker Coonhound! If some time elapses, the rescue will want to know if any of the information on the application has changed, especially if you have moved.

The Adoption Process

Once you have located your Treeing Walker Coonhound, you will need to fill out an adoption application. Usually the application will be on the rescue website. Although each rescue may have different criteria, for the most part, there are standard questions they will ask so they can get to know you and determine what type of home you will provide for your coonhound.

General adoption application questions usually include the following questions:

- Your name and address
- Are you at least 18 years of age?

- Do you live in a house or apartment?
- How long have you lived there?
- Do you have a fenced yard?
- What type of fence?
- Will the dog be indoors/outdoors or both?
- What type of shelter will your outdoor dog have?
- Will your dog have access to fresh water all of the time?
- What type of dog food will you feed him/her?
- Will your dog get exercise?
- What is the name of your veterinarian?
- How many hours will the dog spend alone?
- Do you have other pets, and if so, what kind?
- Are your other pets spayed/neutered?
- Do you have children, and if so, what are their ages?
- Have you ever owned a dog before?
- Tell us about pets you have owned and what happened to them.
- Have you ever adopted a dog before?
- Have you ever surrendered a dog to a shelter or rescue before?
- References
- Do you understand the financial responsibilities of owning a dog?
- Do you agree to providing the proper care for the dog (shelter, food, water, veterinary care)?
- Sign the adoption contract, agreeing to the terms and conditions of the rescue organization.

Some rescues may ask to come see your home so they will know what type of environment the coonhound will be in. If that is not feasible, there is a good chance they will look up your house on Google or Zillow. Additionally, the rescue may want to keep in contact with you for a while and perhaps schedule another home visit to check on the welfare of your adopted Treeing Walker Coonhound.

Photo Courtesy of
Donna Holtzclaw

Ask Questions

It is perfectly fine for you to ask questions, too! Your Treeing Walker Coonhound will become a new member of your family so you will want to know as much about him as possible. Some helpful questions/information requests to ask include:

- Does the coonhound get along with other dogs or cats?
- Does the coonhound like children?
- How long has the Treeing Walker Coonhound been at the rescue?
- Was he/she ever adopted and returned? If yes, ask for an explanation.
- How did the rescue acquire the coonhound? i.e. abusive situation, stray, shelter, owner surrender
- Approximate age
- Has the coonhound been on medications or treated for a medical issue? i.e. mange, injuries, illnesses
- Is the Treeing Walker Coonhound negative for heart worms and other parasites?
- Is the coonhound on heartworm preventative?
- Is he on flea and tick preventive medicine?
- Has he been microchipped?
- Anything else that you think of to ask
- Is there a "trial period" for the dog, providing a full refund if the coonhound needs to be returned?

Meet and Greet

Once you have found your Treeing Walker Coonhound and you have been approved for adoption, a Meet and Greet can be arranged. It may be at a neutral place, if the rescue does not have an actual shelter or facility. The Meet and Greet could be at the foster parent's home, if applicable. The Meet and Greet should, if at all possible, take place in familiar surroundings for the coonhound.

Health Certifications

When you get your Treeing Walker Coonhound from a rescue or animal shelter, your new friend will have been spayed or neutered, be up-to-date on vaccinations, and possibly microchipped. If the dog is older than six months, he will have been checked for heartworms. Dogs from abusive and neglectful situations may have had other surgeries or received treatment for issues such as worms and mange.

Regardless of how much a rescue spends on a dog, the costs are not passed on to you. Rescues normally have a specified adoption fee, which usually (barely) covers the veterinary expenses for vaccinations and spay/neuter surgery. Any additional expenses needed for the dog will be absorbed by the rescue organization. Animal rescues are definitely not rescuing dogs because it is a money-maker. If you can afford it, give the rescue a little extra money with your adoption fee. Believe it or not, an extra $10.00 will help.

*Photo Courtesy of
Sara Bartek*

Occasionally, a rescue will adopt out a dog that still requires medical care. The new owner will be made aware of this and must agree to it. That was what I did with Bowie. He had heartworms and the rescue couldn't afford the fast-kill treatment. I adopted him and put him on the long-term regimen. He is now heartworm-free!

The rescue or shelter will give you a record of your dog's vaccinations, and a health certificate (especially if your coonhound is coming from another state) which also certifies that they have been spayed/neutered. If your coonhound is microchipped, that information will be included as well. Registering your dog's microchip will be a small annual expense. The rabies tag will be sent with the dog so you can pick out a nice collar and attach the "jewelry." If the dog is on medicines, such as antibiotics, the rescue will send that with you, too.

Adoption Return Policy

Animal rescue groups want nothing more than to place a dog in his for-ever, happy home. The dogs are evaluated regarding their temperaments, ability to get along with other dogs and/or children, cats, and people. If it is discovered, perhaps through the foster parents, that a rescue dog prefers to be an only dog, or perhaps was abused or taunted by kids, thereby not trusting kids, the rescue agency will tell potential adopters this, as well as other pertinent information regarding the dog and his history. Many times, if the dog was taken in as a stray, there may not be much history that is known about her. Breed characteristics may help determine how the dog will act.

The adoption papers are a contract with the rescue agency. Signing the adoption papers indicates that you are agreeing to their terms and condi-tions. When you adopt your Treeing Walker Coonhound from an animal rescue, there will be a clause in the adoption papers regarding returning the dog to the rescue should you not be able to care for him. Animal shelters may have this agreement in their contract as well.

Special Coonhound Delivery

Once everything is approved, stamped, paid for, and ready to go, it is time for you to get your new family member! The rescue organization may arrange for transportation to you, at their expense, but give them some extra money if possible. If you live nearby, you can arrange to go and get your hound. If the dog has been in foster care, many times the foster parent will bring the coonhound to you. The rescue organization wants the coonhound to have the least amount of stress as possible in this new transition. However, as I discovered with Casey and Bowie, Treeing Walker Coonhounds are very adaptable and there should not be too much of a problem, if any, with you going to get your coonhound. The drive home will give you some extra bonding time.

Update the Rescue About Your Treeing Walker Coonhound

When animal rescues adopt out dogs, they love nothing better than to be provided updates about the amazing lives the dogs are now living. When you take your Treeing Walker Coonhound home, send periodic updates to the rescue organization. Include photos of your coonhound sleeping on the couch, taking walks, playing with toys, and snuggling with his new family. Many rescues will post these updates on their social media pages as "happy tails" or success stories. Your Treeing Walker Coonhound is now living the good life, so share it!

Some Baggage May Be Included

As I've touched on, if you are rescuing a Treeing Walker Coonhound that is older, there is a good possibility that your coonhound suffered abuse or neglect and that is how he ended up at the rescue.

Hopefully, the trauma that your Treeing Walker Coonhound experienced will become distant memories. Once your coonhound becomes part of your family, he usually will have no problem settling in with you. Preferably on the couch. With a blanket.

Any rescue/adopted animal needs time to get familiar with her new family. Average time for this "honeymoon" is two to three months. It may be shorter; it may be longer. If physical abuse was rampant, your Treeing Walker Coonhound may have some serious trust issues and you will probably need to hire a professional dog trainer to help you and your coonhound through this difficult time and to help establish trust. Perhaps your Treeing Walker Coonhound was kept outdoors so becoming an inside dog might take some time, especially with house training. Don't get angry with your hound. Avoid overstimulating your hound. She is adjusting to her new life, so your job is to be patient and kind. She may have never had a toy to play with or a dog bed to sleep on, so don't get frustrated if she doesn't play immediately or lay on her bed.

The best thing to do for your rescued Treeing Walker Coonhound is to just be there for him. Love him. Have patience. A loving home may be a very new thing for your coonhound. Treeing Walker Coonhounds are pack hounds. Once your new friend realizes that you are now his pack, he will probably adjust to life with you in no time. Casey and Bowie took approximately 30 minutes to fit in.

Foster a Treeing Walker Coonhound

There is also a way to "try before you buy." It is called fostering. In order to foster a coonhound, you will need to fill out an application similar to the adoption application. Many times, the form is the same; you simply check the "foster" box. There are so many benefits to fostering, for you and the Treeing Walker Coonhound. When you foster a dog from a rescue, you become that dog's family and her way of learning how to be a part of a family. You give the dog a home and love and food and attention. She gives you back love and trust and acceptance.

The rescue organization will provide dog food for your coonhound. If medical issues develop, they will cover the cost of the vet bills, too. However, if you purchase the dog food yourself, and take care of minor vet bills (if applicable), I guarantee you that the rescue will appreciate it very much. This counts as a donation and you can deduct it on your taxes.

Fostering can last as long as it takes to find the coonhound a permanent home or may be only for a day or two before the coonhound goes to meet a long-term foster parent or her forever home. Fostering will give you some extra insight and first-hand knowledge of the wonderful world of Treeing Walker Coonhounds.

Coonhound Rescues

I mentioned earlier that there are breed-specific rescues. Treeing Walker Coonhound rescue sites as well as other rescues devoted to all breeds of hound dogs can be found online. There are a few hound rescues I am familiar with and I follow them on Facebook. If you have contact with a local rescue, let them know that you want a Treeing Walker Coonhound. They will be able to network to find one just for you.

Here are a few rescues I am familiar with, check them out in your search for your Treeing Walker Coonhound. Good Luck finding your new friend!

Organization	State	Website
Animal Rescue League of Okemah	OK	arlorescue.org
Diane's Oklahoma Hound Dog Rescue	OK	Facebook Group
3 Girls Animal Rescue, Inc.	OK	3girlsanimalrescue.com
Helpless Hounds Dog Rescue in Tulsa	OK	helplesshounds.com
Horse and Hound Rescue	OK	horseandhoundrescue.com
All Hounds on Deck	LA	allhoundsondeck.com
Coonhound and Foxhound Companions	TX	coonhoundcompanions.com
Coonhounds Needing Rescue!	Nationwide	Facebook Group
Old Friends Senior Dog Sanctuary	TN	ofsds.org
Gentle Jake's Coonhound Rescue	Ontario, Canada	coonhoundrescue.ca
Operation Helping Hounds	West Coast	operationhelpinghounds.org
Priceless Pet Rescue	Nationwide	pricelesspetrescue.org

CHAPTER 4

Buy From A Reputable Breeder

If you have decided on getting a Treeing Walker Coonhound puppy, and the rescues you have checked don't have puppies, it is time to find a reputable Treeing Walker Coonhound breeder.

Research the Breeder

When you search for Treeing Walker Coonhound puppies on the internet, you will probably be able to find puppies in your state or at least in a state near you. Click on as many sites as you can. Additionally, there are hunting dog magazines as well as dog breed magazines, such as Dog Fancy, that feature specific breeds each month. You should be able to find a Treeing Walker Coonhound breeder in the advertising sections of these magazines.

Check for the breeder's history. See how long they have been breeding Treeing Walker Coonhounds. Find out if the parents are show dogs, hunting dogs, or perhaps both. If you plan on showing your Treeing Walker Coonhound in dog shows or coonhound trials, determine if the puppies have AKC registration papers.

FUN FACT
Recognized by the AKC

Treeing Walker Coonhounds were officially recognized by the AKC in 2012, making them the sixth Coonhound to be recognized by that organization. TWCs were also the 175th breed overall to be recognized by the AKC.

Another way to find a reputable breeder is to attend a dog show. Puppies cannot be sold at AKC shows, but you will have a chance to observe Treeing Walker Coonhounds. Walking around behind the scenes will provide you an opportunity to meet the breeder and talk to them. You will also get to meet and greet their Treeing Walker Coonhounds, which may be the potential parents of your puppy.

If you want to delve into the world of dog shows, then AKC papers will be necessary and important for this. If you have no interest in showing and breeding your Treeing Walker Coonhound, AKC papers, in my opinion, are irrelevant.

From what I've seen in internet searches, a Treeing Walker Coonhound puppy will cost around $500.00; maybe a little more, maybe a little less. If the puppy is not near you, then you will incur traveling expenses. I think it is imperative that you let your Treeing Walker Coonhound puppy pick you for her family. So, if it is possible, visit the breeding facilities. More on that later.

Many of the dogs that make their way to shelters and rescues, are the result of cruel backyard breeders and overbreeding. The bitches are bred twice/year, when they come into heat. Males on the other hand, can be bred to as many females in heat as they come in contact with. Many times, the health and life of the dog is not factored in. Churning out dogs, healthy or not, to make money, is the motivation.

However, there are reputable breeders who don't have a commercial breeding facility for show dogs. They simply love the breed.

Usually, small-time or part-time breeders will sell their puppies cheaper than a well-established, show-quality breeder. If you happen to get the last puppy, or maybe they have a pup from a previous litter (if you want a pup that is six months old or so), the price may be even cheaper.

Visit the Breeding Facilities

Whichever breeder you decide to get your puppy from, be sure that you visit the facilities if possible. Make this a priority. More than likely, you won't have a choice to not go and get your puppy from the facility as small-time breeders may not want to deal with transporting your puppy to you if you live out-of-state.

You can learn a lot about possible or potential health issues your Treeing Walker Coonhound might have by looking at their environment. Even though this breed is relatively healthy in general, health issues that may develop might not be genetic, but rather environmental. Fresh, clean water should be available for the dogs, as well as adequate shelter. The dogs should be relatively clean (unless there is a mud puddle nearby) and free of ticks and fleas.

While a local, small-time breeder probably doesn't have a place set up for a full veterinary practice or have training/showing facilities, you will be able to see if the place is neat and clean. Dog poop should be minimal. Kennels should be washed and clean. Runs and yards should be well-kept and tidy. That's not to say that if you see one pile of dog poop that you should get in your car and leave. Dogs poop. Dogs pee. But if there are piles and piles of feces and/or puddles and puddles of urine, along with the pungent smell of the excess waste, it is obvious that hygiene isn't one of the breeder's top priorities. You might need to find another place to get your Treeing Walker Coonhound puppy.

If the breeder has other dogs, you can see how their health is. The stud may be on-site so make it a point to meet him as well as the mother.

Photo Courtesy of
Suzanne M. Stierwalt

Should you decide to get your puppy from a larger, professional breeder, still visit the facilities. Just because they are bigger doesn't mean that they are better. These breeders should be willing to give you a tour of their facilities. There may be a room full of trophies and photos that they will be happy to show you, too. They might have older pups or dogs from the same mother or father, or perhaps siblings of the parents as well, so ask if you can meet them. This will help you get a good idea of what your dog's disposition should be like.

Ask Questions

Ask a lot of questions! Find out as much about the breeder and their coonhounds as you can.

- How long have they been breeding Treeing Walker Coonhounds?
- Are the parents on the premises?
- Can you meet the parents?
- Can you meet other dogs on the premises?
- If you don't plan on showing your coonhound, ask if they have puppies that aren't "show quality" but will be a great member of your family. The breeder may be happy to reduce the price if the puppy isn't show or breeding quality.
- Are there any health issues you should be concerned about (genetic, environmental)?
- Do the puppies have AKC papers?
- Have they had their first set of shots?
- Have they been wormed?
- What kind of food have the puppies been eating?
- Do they guarantee the health of the dog?
- Is there a time frame (days, weeks) for the health guarantee, barring any accidents?
- Is there a return policy?
- Is there a time frame for returning the puppy?
- If the puppy is returned, is there a full refund?
- Is the return policy specific for certain health exceptions, or is it a "no questions asked" policy?

What to Look For in a Treeing Walker Coonhound Puppy

After you have investigated the facilities and asked questions (you can always ask questions as you think of them), it is time to look at the Treeing Walker Coonhound puppies! Hound puppies are about as cute as they come, so be prepared to fall in love with all of them.

To avoid a little bit of heartache when you go to get your puppy, ask the breeder to keep the puppies that are already spoken for (if applicable) separated from the available puppies. Why? Because the odds are great that you will fall in love with a puppy that already has a new family waiting for him. Or her. Which brings up another point.

If you want a male puppy, have the breeder keep the females separate. Same thing if you absolutely must have a female.

Sit down among the puppies. Let them crawl and tumble and snuggle on you. While they are doing this, pick them up one at a time. Look into their wrinkly little face. Their eyes should be bright, clear, and dark brown. Make sure there is no matter or mucous coming out of their eyes and that they don't appear to be sensitive to light or in pain.

As the puppies run around, watch their gaits. It should be fluid and smooth, even while they are bouncing around. Check for limping or soreness.

Look in their floppy ears and make sure they are a healthy pink without redness or excessive dirt. Their mama is probably still giving them daily baths, too, and cleaning their ears.

Check their gums to make sure that they are a healthy pink and not whitish.

Coonhounds have excess skin. Check their skin to make sure it is loose, pliable, and healthy. You should be able to gently pull on the skin without causing any distress or pain to the puppy.

The puppies should have little round bellies from being well-fed. A little roundness is okay and should be in line with their bodies and height. However, you don't want to see a distended belly, which could indicate illness or worms.

Treeing Walker Coonhound puppies should be alert and happy little puppies. More than likely you will be surrounded by them, but notice if any of them tend to stay to themselves. Spend some time with that puppy as he may warm up to you and start wagging his tail. It could be shyness or maybe he is the runt. Be sure and ask the breeder if the puppy is okay.

Look around for any signs of diarrhea. This includes checking the rear ends of the puppies.

Unless puppies are sleeping, their tails should be wagging constantly or erect as they play and go on patrol. You might even hear a coonhound puppy bark or howl!

Listen for excessive coughing, wheezing, and sneezing. Coonhound puppy noses should be free from runny discharge.

Prepare to be sniffed. Coonhounds are scent hounds and this is part of their genetics. They will smell everything!

Once you have established that the litter of coonhound puppies is healthy and happy and you have exhausted the breeder with questions, it is time to pick your puppy. Rather, to be more correct, it is time to let the puppy pick you!

Chosen By a Treeing Walker Coonhound Puppy

Picking out your puppy actually turns into letting the puppy pick you! While you are spending time with the puppies, pay close attention to which puppy (or puppies) is spending time with you.

When we got Baloo, my Great Pyrenees, I was pregnant with my second son. I called and scheduled an appointment to "look" at the puppies. Yeah. There were four puppies I believe, as well as their mother, onsite. Four little balls of white fluff were running around the large yard. The mother took our visit as an opportunity for some quality Me Time and found a shady spot to lay down.

I sat down on the grass with Ian. David stood next to me while the puppies tumbled around us. One puppy promptly crawled into my lap and Ian and I began petting him. The others soon ran off, discovering that their mother was somehow managing to exist without them. The puppy in my lap didn't even attempt to go with them. My decision was made. Baloo picked out Ian. He picked out me. He picked out David and I like to think that he even picked out Justin, who was growing inside me.

The puppy may pick you right away, perhaps as soon as you enter their enclosure. Maybe it will take a little longer as you spend time with them. More than likely, there will be one puppy that wants to spend all of his time with you. Trust that this is the one for you. Knowing that you were selected, chosen, by a dog, is a wonderful feeling. It is an absolute honor.

Avoid Pet Stores and Flea Markets

Avoid purchasing your Treeing Walker Coonhound puppy from a pet store or flea market. Chances are that the puppies sold in these places come from puppy mills/backyard breeders, as discussed earlier, where the dogs are monetized and their health and happiness isn't cared for at all.

Pet stores will jack the prices of these dogs up dramatically. Puppies priced at $1000, or more, are the norm. And congenital conditions, diseases, abnormalities, and deformities may not present themselves for a while, though they're almost certain to appear due to the dogs' poor start in life.

Buy from a reputable breeder or adopt a Treeing Walker Coonhound. It is just that simple.

Photo Courtesy of
Mary Dugan

AKC Treeing Walker Coonhound Breeders

If the breeder you are interested in is a designated AKC breeder, the AKC has recommended health tests for each particular breed. For Treeing Walker Coonhounds the AKC recommends:

- A hip evaluation
- An ophthalmologist evaluation
- A thyroid evaluation

Certain AKC breeders of Treeing Walker Coonhounds may have an AKC BOM, or Breeder of Merit, symbol on their website.

To achieve Breeder of Merit status, the breeder has proven their dedication to preserving the breed characteristics of the Treeing Walker Coonhound, does everything they can to produce litters with optimal health and temperament, certifies they have performed the applicable health screens for their Treeing Walker Coonhound puppies, and that they have provided the proper care and socialization of their puppies. Breeders of Merit must have a minimum of four dogs that have earned titles. Levels for Breeders of Merit are Standard, Bronze, Silver, Gold and Platinum.

Another AKC program for breeders is the Bred With H.E.A.R.T. (health, education, accountability, responsibility, and tradition). AKC breeders make a commitment to follow the program requirements for the health and well-being of their purebred Treeing Walker Coonhounds.

- **HEALTH**: Breeders certify that their breeding stock is health-tested according to the AKC Breed Parent Club recommendations for Treeing Walker Coonhounds.
- **EDUCATION:** Breeders promise that they will pursue or continue with AKC breeder education and will stay current on the best breeding practices and advancements in canine health.
- **ACCOUNTABILITY:** AKC has Care and Conditions Policies and breeders must comply with them, allowing AKC inspections of their kennels as well as sharing health testing and continuing education achievements and documentations with the AKC.
- **RESPONSIBILITY:** Breeders assume the responsibility for the health of their puppies and compliance with the laws for the ownership, care and maintenance of their Treeing Walker Coonhounds.
- **TRADITION:** Breeders must uphold the AKC's tradition of breeding purebred dogs that are happy and healthy.

Health Certification Guarantee and Return Policy

Once your Treeing Walker Coonhound puppy has chosen you and you are ready to take her to her new home, it is time for the paperwork.

Many breeders, large or small, offer health guarantees for their puppies. This may be included in a bill of sale or be a separate item. Breeders who are serious about their businesses and reputations will want the health of their puppies to be their top priority.

Each breeder may have their own specific health guarantee or they may have downloaded one from the internet. Regardless, the health guarantee should include the following:

- Proof of vaccinations for puppies 6-8 weeks old.
- Proof of worming medication administered to the puppy.
- Buyer will have a veterinarian give the puppy a health examination within a certain timeframe from the purchase of the puppy.
- Seller does not reimburse buyer for the veterinarian exam.
- If a serious disease or defect is discovered, the seller may offer a replacement puppy (if one is available) or a full refund.
- Breed-specific or life-threatening diseases/conditions may be outlined and covered (replacement or refund) for up to one year.
- Non-breed-specific issues, such as cherry eye, that are not covered by the breeder.
- Buyer must provide proof of the health condition from the veterinarian.
- Seller may require a second veterinary opinion.
- Buyer agrees to provide proper care for the coonhound.
- Spaying/Neutering policy may be included if the buyer does not plan to breed or show the coonhound.
- Other clauses that are related to specific experiences from the seller.
- The health guarantee may be voided if buyer fails to properly care for the coonhound and/or notify the seller within the allotted time if health issues arise.

If the breeder, large or small, happens to be a veterinarian, and if you live nearby, the veterinarian/breeder might offer to care for your dog at a reduced rate as well.

If the small, local breeders don't actually have a written health guarantee, be sure and ask questions. They may administer worming medicine before you take your puppy home and the puppies may have already had their first set of vaccinations. This will be included in the price of the puppy, but you need to find out if your coonhound puppy has had, or needs, vaccinations and worming.

Photo Courtesy of Nancy Vermaat

More than likely, the larger breeding facilities will offer a return policy. This may or may not be included in the health guarantee. Top breeders may have a policy to take the puppy back under any and all circumstances. Small breeders may offer these guarantees, too, so be sure that you ask.

Before we got our basset hound puppy, Bridgette, we actually had bought a basset hound puppy from another breeder. We had the veterinarian do a health check on our puppy and the vet found some things that he was concerned about. We contacted the breeder and she took the puppy back and refunded our money. So be sure you check with small breeders. If they have been in the business for a long time, they want to keep their good reputations going and don't want to be known for selling sickly puppies. They should also be concerned about the life their puppy will have, so if it turns out that a calamity strikes and you aren't able to care for the puppy, they should accept it back. Again, it is okay to ask them about a health guarantee and return policy.

CHAPTER 5

Raising a Treeing Walker Coonhound Puppy

Congratulations! You are the proud owner of a Treeing Walker Coonhound puppy! The fun is about to begin!

Photo Courtesy of Danica Schiller

Cuteness Overload

You might have heard the expression "as cute as a speckled pup." Well, as the proud owner of a Treeing Walker Coonhound puppy, you can guess where that expression came from because hound puppies are just about the cutest things in the world.

As you discovered when you and your puppy picked out each other, Treeing Walker Coonhound puppies are a mixture of floppy ears, some really cute wrinkles, spots and speckles, big brown eyes, big feet that they will grow into, and a nose that never stops working.

This curious, sniffing bundle of joy will bring you years of happiness and laughter. You will probably never cease to be amazed at your new member of the family.

Puppy Teeth and Puppy Breath

Your Treeing Walker Coonhound will not start developing teeth until he is about two weeks old. His incisors will erupt first, followed by pre-molars, molars, and canine teeth. By the time your coonhound puppy is six or seven weeks old, he should have 28 milk teeth.

When you bring your Treeing Walker Coonhound puppy home, he should be between six and eight weeks old. You will get to experience the awesome smell of puppy breath! Maybe it's the combination of the mother's milk and the fact that the puppy has not yet eaten anything that he should not have eaten. I don't know. But I do know that the smell is universal for puppies, and everyone seems to love "puppy breath."

At around eight weeks, the milk teeth begin to fall out, making way for the permanent teeth to begin arriving around the age of 12 weeks. This is a good time to invest in a sturdy, hard plastic chew toy for your puppy. Anything, including your fine, expensive leather boots or shoes, will be fair game for your coonhound to relieve the pressures of teething. Keep your shoes and any other delectable items picked up and stored in another room. The teething phase won't last forever, so make it more pleasant for both of you by getting your coonhound puppy appropriate teething toys.

By the time your Treeing Walker Coonhound is seven months old, he should have all 42 of his permanent teeth. The upper jaw (maxilla) will have 20 teeth and the lower jaw, the mandible, will have 22 teeth.

House Training

Treeing Walker Coonhounds are exceptionally intelligent. Because of this, house training your puppy should not take too long, perhaps just a few days or maybe a couple of weeks.

Probably the easiest way to house train your puppy will be to take him out every hour or two if you are able. Familiarize your coonhound puppy with the backdoor, so he knows this is the way outside to relieve himself. If it's an emergency, carry the puppy out and set him down. If you have time, let him follow you out the back door. Once he is outside, let him sniff around and find a spot to do his business. Praise him, starting with his name and then tell him he's a good boy. Your puppy will get the hang of it.

If you get your puppy during the winter and there is a bunch of snow on the ground, you might need to resort to potty pads. Put them by your back door so your coonhound will begin to associate the back door with going outside to go to the bathroom.

More than likely, there will be accidents. When your puppy has an accident, do not ever rub his nose in his waste or spank him. We don't potty train our kids that way. It reinforces negativity and fear that your coonhound will associate with you and also with going to the bathroom. It could build up some resentment. Simply pick up your puppy as soon as you see him have a little accident and take him outside. Even though he has already peed or pooped, he will get the idea. He may not be finished either, so if he goes to the bathroom again outside, give him some praise and pet him.

One simple way to help avoid any accidents is to watch your puppy. When your little Treeing Walker Coonhound needs to go to the bathroom, he will start sniffing around. Although puppies are almost always sniffing, you will be able to tell if he's just sniffing your couch or shoes or a new toy, or if he's walking around, maybe hunching over a little, searching for a place to relieve himself. When you see this, take the puppy outside.

I had a veterinarian tell me years ago to take my puppy to the same place in the yard. Sometimes it might not be feasible if your puppy has to go right now and the "toilet" is on the other side of the yard. However, it is a good habit and makes picking up the yard much easier than looking for piles of poop throughout the yard.

When you see your puppy squatting in your house, try to refrain from yelling, "NO!" We tend to use the word "no" for everything, such as

Photo Courtesy of Kevin Thibault

getting in the trash, jumping up on someone, using the bathroom in the house, chewing on things, or a host of any other undesirable activities. It's hard to not yell "NO!" But as we will discuss later, you should try to use a different word for each activity you are training your Treeing Walker Coonhound to do or not do.

For instance, since your puppy needs to go outside to pee, you might simply say, "Pee" or "Go Pee" and put your puppy outside. Reinforcing that word with the action of going outside let's your coonhound know that this is acceptable behavior and he will get some positive reinforcement when he performs well.

You might write down a list of simple word commands or cues that you want to use and start practicing them with your puppy.

Vaccinations/Worming

Puppies need to get their very first oral worming medications at two weeks of age and repeated at four weeks. If your Treeing Walker Coonhound is six to eight weeks old when you get him, he may or may not have had his first set of vaccinations, but he should definitely be ready for another round of worm medications. He will need the vaccinations for distemper and parvovirus.

- Distemper is a contagious airborne virus that spreads from sneezing, coughing, or using the same water/food bowls. It causes dogs to have a discharge from their eyes and noses, as well as vomiting, fever, coughing, diarrhea, seizures, hardened foot pads, twitching, paralysis, and can be fatal.

- Parvovirus is a highly contagious virus. Puppies under the age of four months are at a high risk of contracting it if they aren't vaccinated. The virus affects the gastrointestinal tract, causing a loss of appetite, severe vomiting, and bloody diarrhea. The virus can cause extreme dehydration and may be fatal within 48-72 hours.

- Bordatella is highly infectious, causing coughing, whooping, vomiting, and possibly seizures and death. It causes kennel cough. The vaccine can be injected or be administered as a nasal spray. If your puppy is going to stay at home, you won't have to get the vaccine until later. If you need to board your puppy for some reason, want to introduce him to doggy day care, or begin a training program, your Treeing Walker Coonhound puppy will then definitely have to be vaccinated for Bordatella.

- Kennel Cough can be a bacterial or viral infection. The upper airways become infected and inflamed, causing harsh, dry coughing, retching, gagging, and a loss of appetite. It is easily spread throughout kennels and can lead to death in certain cases.

- Roundworms affect nearly all dogs at some point in their lives as they are the most common canine worm. They can spread from the mother to the puppies while the puppies are still in utero or after birth through the mother's milk. Roundworms live in the intestines and cause vomiting, diarrhea, weight loss, and a pot-belly. Roundworms can migrate to the coonhound's lungs and induce coughing. You will be able to see the whitish-colored worms in your coonhound's poop, so while you are picking up poop from the yard, check for worms. Roundworms can be transmitted to humans, so use protective equipment such as disposable gloves when you are cleaning up your coonhound's poop if you know or

Photo Courtesy of
Rebecca Cummins

suspect that he has roundworms. Always wash your hands after handling dog poop, whether worms are present or not.

- Tapeworms can also live in your Treeing Walker Coonhound's intestines. They are large, flat worms and you will know that your coonhound has them if you notice small, white worms about the size of a grain of rice on your hound's rear end, in his poop, or even in his bed. Humans can also be infected with tapeworms, although they are rare in the United States.

- Hookworms attach to the lining of the intestines and consume your coonhound's blood. Their eggs are laid in the intestines and are eliminated when your dog poops. Then they live in the soil and any dog who licks the soil can be infected. Hookworms can be fatal to puppies by causing blood loss. In addition to blood loss, adult dogs can experience diarrhea and weight loss. Humans walking barefoot through soil contaminated with hookworms can contract them as well.

- Whipworms live in the cecum of your Treeing Walker Coonhound, where the large and small intestines connect. Your coonhound may have bloody diarrhea, and a severe infection of whipworms can be fatal to your hound. Humans can also be infected with whipworms by handling/ingesting contaminated soil through playing in the dirt or gardening or eating food that is not properly cleaned.

- Heartworms are a serious health concern that will be discussed in Chapter 12. Puppies are not normally infected with heartworms, but when your Treeing Walker Coonhound puppy is six months old, you should start having him checked for heartworms, which are transmitted through mosquito bites. Talk to your veterinarian about a heartworm preventative for your Treeing Walker Coonhound puppy.

When your Treeing Walker Coonhound puppy is 10-12 weeks old, she will need a second set of vaccinations for distemper and parvovirus as well as the first vaccinations for hepatitis and parainfluenza. This set of vaccinations is referred to as DHPP. He will need to be wormed again, too.

- Hepatitis, or adenovirus, affects the kidneys, liver, spleen, lungs and even the eyes of dogs. It is highly contagious, causing jaundice, enlargement of the stomach, pain around the liver, vomiting, and congestion of the mucous membranes and a fever.

- Parainfluenza is one of the viruses that causes kennel cough. If your coonhound has not had the Bordatella vaccine, he can get it now.

- Your veterinarian might also recommend vaccinating your coonhound puppy against Influenza, Leptospirosis, and Lyme disease.

- Canine Influenza is an airborne dog flu caused by influenza A and affects the respiratory tract. H3N8 and H3N2 are the strains that infect dogs. It may be spread through contact with other dogs or objects such as food/water bowls or toys that have been contaminated, as well as kennels, doggy day care centers, dog parks, and grooming salons. An infected dog can bark or cough onto another dog, spreading the virus. Dogs are contagious for up to ten days after exposure. Dogs may be asymptomatic, but can still be contagious. Canine influenza is not seasonal. Dogs exhibit coughing, sneezing, a nasal discharge, runny eyes, fever, lethargy, and difficulty breathing.

- Leptospirosis are a bacteria, found in soil and water, that can spread from animals to humans. Fever, vomiting, abdominal pain, diarrhea, loss of appetite, lethargy, weakness, jaundice, stiffness, muscle pain, infertility, and kidney failure can be symptoms of infection.

- Lyme Disease is a tick-borne disease. Dogs with Lyme Disease will begin limping, their lymph nodes swell, their temperature rises, and there is a loss of appetite. Lyme Disease can lead to neurological disorders and affect the heart, liver, and joints. Ticks and fleas will be discussed in Chapter 12.

At 16-18 weeks of age, your Treeing Walker Coonhound puppy will need his second DHPP vaccinations and first set of rabies vaccinations. If your puppy did not get vaccinated for Influenza, Leptospirosis or Lyme Disease, you might also get him vaccinated for those diseases.

- Rabies is a viral infection that attacks the central nervous system, usually transmitted through the bite of an infected animal. Rabies can cause headaches, anxiety, hallucinations, excessive drooling, paralysis, fear of water, and it almost always eventually causes the death of the infected animal. Your state and city/town may require a rabies vaccination annually or every other year. Check with your veterinarian about the schedule for your coonhound. If you plan to hunt with your Treeing Walker Coonhound, you definitely need to get your hound vaccinated for rabies.

- Coronavirus in dogs affects their gastrointestinal system. It is not the same coronavirus that causes COVID-19 in humans. A coonhound with coronavirus will experience a loss of appetite, vomiting, and diarrhea.

If you do not plan on breeding or showing your Treeing Walker Coonhound, please have your puppy spayed or neutered at six months of age. The recovery from these surgeries is relatively quick and easy and eliminates the worry of any unwanted litters. If your Treeing Walker Coonhound has AKC papers and you plan on showing him, then your coonhound must be intact. Bitches in heat will need to be confined and intact males should never be allowed to roam free.

Microchipping

When you take your Treeing Walker Coonhound for any shots, you should also have your veterinarian microchip him. A tiny, grain-of-rice-sized identification transponder is inserted between your coonhound's shoulder blades. The tiny transponder is actually a radio-frequency identification transponder with its own identification number. The identification number is transmitted when the hound is scanned for a microchip.

You will need to register your Treeing Walker Coonhound's microchip number with a microchip tracking company and pay a small annual fee. Once the number is activated, the number can be checked with databases by veterinarians or rescue organizations. Your personal information, particularly your name, address and all applicable phone numbers will be retrieved, and this allows you to be notified of your coonhound's whereabouts should he get separated from you. Then you and your hound can be reunited.

If your Treeing Walker Coonhound has AKC registration paper, the AKC has a program called AKC Reunite. You can enroll in this program and register your hound's microchip number with the AKC, which provides a Lost Pet Alert that broadcasts your coonhound's information to veterinarians and animal shelters in your area. The AKC will send you a custom AKC collar tag (more jewelry!) with their toll-free pet recovery phone number on it. Your contact information and your hound's microchip ID number are linked to AKC Reunite. When your dog is found, AKC Reunite will contact you as soon as possible! There is no charge for this service so if your puppy has AKC papers, it would be wise to add this extra protection for your coonhound.

Safeguarding Your Home and Yard

Although securing your home and yard was discussed in Chapter 2, now that you have your Treeing Walker Coonhound puppy, it would behoove you to do periodic evaluations of your house and yard.

Spend extra time with your puppy and follow him around the yard. It's a great sniffing and exploration opportunity for your coonhound puppy. You can do another inspection to see if there are any holes in the fence or dangerous things your puppy might decide to snack on. Pay attention to what your coonhound puppy is most interested in. For example, he may decide that the tiny little hole by the fence that he discovered will need to be excavated later.

Picking up the dog poop is also a good time to do a quick inventory of your yard. Let your Treeing Walker Coonhound puppy follow you around.

Photo Courtesy of Brooke and Ben Newell

This makes a good opportunity for him to "use the facilities" and get some more high praise from you.

If you have a swimming pool, do not leave your coonhound puppy unattended in the yard. It will be very easy for him to toddle into the pool. However, getting in the pool with him when he is a little older and showing him where the steps are would be very beneficial for him.

Inside your house, get down on the floor with your puppy and see what he might see, sniff, or eat. As your puppy grows, things once tucked away in a "safe" place might not be safe anymore and will need to be relocated. Ensure that all electrical cords and outlets are covered/protected and monitor your Treeing Walker Coonhound puppy to ensure that he doesn't consider cords part of his toy collection.

As your coonhound puppy grows, coffee tables, and things on top of them, become more easily accessible. Their corners may provide a great place to chew and sharpen teeth. It goes without saying that anything that occupies space on the coffee table, such as magazines, books, television remotes, coasters, or breakable items, could become the victim of a Treeing Walker Coonhound mouth or wagging tail.

Food For Your Treeing Walker Coonhound Puppy

Your Treeing Walker Coonhound puppy will need a healthy and balanced diet. This can be found in a high-quality puppy food, recommended by the breeder or your veterinarian. Your coonhound puppy will need the appropriate daily amounts of vitamins and minerals, as well as proteins for his tissues, carbohydrates for energy, and healthy fats for his hair, skin, coat, eyes, and brain.

Follow the recommended amounts of food listed on the package to give to your coonhound puppy. He will need to be fed several times per day until he is at least a year old. Treeing Walker Coonhound puppies that are two to three months old will need to be fed four times/day. When they are three to six months old, they need to be fed three times per day. At 6-12 months, feed your hound twice/day.

It is important to leave your coonhound puppy alone while he eats. This is a good idea for a dog of any age or breed, as well as any kind of animal. Mealtime is your coonhound's private time. He needs to know, and be assured, that the food is his and his alone and that no one or no other dog is going to get it. Although hounds are famous for gobbling up their food, barely taking time to chew or taste it, if your little coonhound doesn't have to worry about sharing or getting his food eaten by someone else, there is a chance he might slow down a little while he eats, helping him avoid choking or digestion problems later.

Avoid giving your coonhound puppy table scraps. Greasy, fatty, or sugary foods can upset his little tummy and could be the start of a life-long preference for human food, creating the bad habit of begging.

Healthy treats may be given sporadically throughout the day. However, note that they are additional calories and can add up to increased weight gain quickly. Your

FUN FACT
What is Treeing?

Treeing is a hunting method where dogs chase naturally climbing prey into trees, where prey can then be assessed and shot by hunters. For this technique to work, dogs must not stop barking once the prey has climbed into a tree so that the hunter can determine which tree the prey has climbed. Coonhounds are usually naturally inclined to this behavior, and it's where the Treeing Walker Coonhound gets the "treeing" part of the breed's name. The phrase "barking up the wrong tree" also comes from this hunting method.

Treeing Walker Coonhound will waste no time in discovering where the treat jar is and could get in the habit of expecting (read demanding) a treat to go outside. To come inside. Because he pooped outside. Because he peed outside. Because it is Sunday. Because it is not Sunday. And on and on. You will have to be firm, even with two perked-up floppy ears and two big, brown, marble eyes gazing at you, begging you, imploring you for just one more little treat. Flash your puppy the open hands signal to let him know that that is all there is.

Enjoy your cute little bundle of joy! They grow up so fast!

CHAPTER 6
The Teenage Years

Dog Years

Unfortunately for us, dogs don't live as long as humans. If they did, then we would never be blessed with all of our wonderful canine companions. Smaller dogs live longer than larger dogs. Length of life can vary between breeds as well. Your Treeing Walker Coonhound is considered a large breed.

Considering that the average human lives tend to be at least 80 and your Treeing Walker Coonhound has a lifespan of about 15 years, he will age considerably faster than you do. Your hound will hit middle age when he is six or seven years old. Theoretically, when a human is 50, he has a good 30 years left. Your coonhound has to cram 30 years into seven or eight years.

Photo Courtesy of Rachel Hania

So while you may not notice a big difference between 50 and 51, or even 50 to 55, your Treeing Walker Coonhound will age several years between ages seven to eight and eight to nine.

Treeing Walker Coonhounds have a lot of living to do in their 15 years on earth, so each birthday will age them several more years relative to a human birthday.

If you got your coonhound as a puppy and he is now one year old, or maybe you just rescued a Treeing Walker Coonhound who is one year old, congratulations are in order either way. You have a teenager! Your one-year-old coonhound is equivalent to a 15-year-old human. That is fourteen "dog years." So while a six-month-old coonhound is probably like a seven- or eight-year-old human child, and a one-year-old coonhound is a teenager, the "seven dog years per human year" stops about now. Your two-year-old coonhound has graduated from college and is old enough to vote and live on his own!

Energy

Treeing Walker Coonhounds run the gambit on energy. When they are on the hunt for raccoons, they can run all night. Their stamina makes them great dogs to take on walks or jogs as they can keep up the pace. However, be wise about the temperature of the streets during warmer weather. Hot streets can cause severe burns on your coonhound's foot pads, even after a short walk.

Your Treeing Walker Coonhound will also enjoy exploring the yard so he is fine to leave outside. Coonhounds also very much enjoy curling up or stretching out in a dog bed, your bed, the couch, the floor, or your lap. While they do have energy, I have not found them to be hyperactive.

HELPFUL TIP
Lure Coursing
For Exercise

Lure coursing can be an excellent sport for any dog with a strong prey drive, including Treeing Walker Coonhounds! Based on the ancient sport of chasing small game, lure coursing can be done at a recreational course or practiced in your backyard with a DIY setup. This often-competitive sport requires your dog to chase a mechanized lure in an open area. The AKC and the American Sighthound Field Association (ASFA) are the two sanctioned clubs for lure coursing in America. The Canadian Kennel Club (CKC) and Federation Cynologique Internationale (FCI) oversee competitions in Canada and Europe respectively.

Photo Courtesy of
Albert Treadwell

And while they are intelligent, they do not need the constant stimulation and challenges that a Belgian Malinois or border collie does. Treeing Walker Coonhounds are agile so they enjoy certain agility obstacles. Let your coonhound jump up on trees all that he wants to.

If you have a swimming pool, make sure your coonhound knows how to get out of the pool safely in case he falls in. Casey and Bowie have never shown any interest in getting in the pool. However, accidents do happen and when your coonhound is busy playing, he might accidentally fall in the pool. If you aren't home, he needs to know how to get out of the pool. If you swim with your coonhound, it is a great time to show him. Some coonhounds enjoy swimming in the lake and ocean, and even riding in boats.

Some coonhounds avoid getting in the water at all costs. So if your hound is a water dog, invest in a life jacket for him if you take him out in a boat.

Your Treeing Walker Coonhound will more than likely enjoy playing with children and probably other dogs as well. When Bowie had to be boarded, the weekend kennel tech brought her son to work and Bowie played with him while the woman worked.

Hounds are super friendly and usually respond favorably to children. However you should not leave a young child unattended with your coonhound, especially on the first few meetings. After a few introductory sessions, you can see how it goes. Never allow a child to jump onto your coonhound or climb onto his back to "ride." If your Treeing Walker Coonhound, or any dog for that matter, is sleeping, being startled from his rest by a child jumping on him could cause an instinctive, protective reaction, even including an unintentional bite.

Coonhounds hunt in packs so they are generally used to other dogs. But the same rule applies with introducing your hound to other dogs. It is a good idea to slowly introduce your Treeing Walker Coonhound to other dogs, particularly at a dog park. While your coonhound may behave like a perfect angel, the other dogs may not. Once proper introductions are made, your coonhound should enjoy running and romping with other dogs. Use common sense and caution and things should be fine.

Exercise

As mentioned above, your Treeing Walker Coonhound will have some energy. Daily walks are always an adventure as your coonhound will enjoy spending time with you as well as sniffing just about everything. If you have to squeeze in a short walk due to time restraints, your hound will still enjoy it. If you have the time, take a leisurely walk and let your coonhound sniff and smell everything he can. Observe your coonhound; notice what he smells, how he carries himself. Watch him hold his head up and sniff the air.

Walks at dusk must be carried out with caution since the witching hour for raccoons is near. I took Casey for a walk at dusk once. Once. He spent his time smelling and looking up in every tree we saw (our neighborhood has tons of trees), searching for raccoons. It was a learning curve for me, but it was still a fascinating experience.

Most of the time, your Treeing Walker Coonhound will get plenty of exercise running around the backyard, even if he has to skip his daily walk for some reason. Doggy day care provides an excellent opportunity for playtime and socialization.

Treeing Walker Coonhounds who are in excellent health, including the proper weight, will be able to keep up with almost any activity. You want to make sure that you don't overexercise your hound. On the other hand, too much inactivity can cause your Treeing Walker Coonhound to gain weight. Find a program and schedule that lets you bond with your hound and lets him thrive.

Playtime

Your Treeing Walker Coonhound will enjoy a variety of toys. Stuffed animals with squeakers are great fun. Ripping out the squeaker and the stuffing, plus shaking the daylights out of the toy will let your hound experience the "thrill of the hunt" without actually going on a hunt. Bowie has perfected ripping off the heads, tails, and some legs of all of his stuffed animal toys.

Tug-of-war, whether it is with a rope, a sturdy toy made out of Kevlar, or the tail of an unfortunate, headless, stuffed raccoon, is something your Treeing Walker Coonhound will enjoy. You will discover how strong these dogs are when they are pulling against you. Tug-of-war is also enjoyable with another dog. Be prepared for your dog to bring you a toy to throw or play tug-of-war with during the most serious or sad part of a movie. It is really hard to refuse a big, floppy-eared, marble-eyed hound who wants to have some fun, quality time with you. Pause the movie and enjoy your coonhound.

Treeing Walker Coonhounds are not natural fetchers, but Bowie does enjoy bringing me a toy and having me throw it. He will pounce on it, shake it furiously, and bring it to me for tug-of-war or for me to throw again. He's usually good for four or five fetching sessions, then he will take the toy to his dog bed and chew around on it.

Although your Treeing Walker Coonhound will investigate the scent of anything that has wandered or scurried through the yard, some people discover dead raccoons and drag them around their yard and around trees and up on the trees. When their coonhounds are turned loose, they actually get to follow a real scent and track some game.

If your coonhound plays with toys, make sure that they aren't small enough to swallow and get lodged in the throat or cause a blockage in the stomach or intestines. If your Treeing Walker Coonhound enjoys squeaking toys, be sure to throw the squeakers away as they can be a choking hazard for your hound. It is also super annoying listening to your hound chew on the squeaker so it squeaks and squeaks and squeaks.

Bowie can make a toy out of just about anything. Sticks, roots, large bones, antlers, old pillows, you name it. He even loves to grab one of the numerous dog beds and shake it or drag it around the house. Of course, the stuffing is fun to pull out, too. If you get your coonhound deer antlers to chew on, make sure to throw them away when they are chewed down to a size where pieces can be swallowed.

Another fun thing your Treeing Walker Coonhound will enjoy is discovering treats you have hidden throughout the house (in rooms where he is allowed) or yard. Since you have a scent hound and his wonderful nose will be discussed in detail in Chapter 8, you can drag the treat around the house until you find a hiding place for it. Your hound will probably follow the trail to get his reward. I would place the treats in easy-to-reach places, such as on top of an end table or in a corner of the room. If you stuff treats between your couch cushions, that smell will stay there and you coonhound will always "hunt" for the treats, which could mean chewed-up couch cushions.

Photo Courtesy of
Danica Schiller

Many dogs rip their stuffed toys to shreds, so you can take an old sock, put a treat in it, tie a knot in the end and give it to your coonhound. It won't take him long to get the treat and he will have a good time.

Food for Your Treeing Walker Coonhound

You fed your puppy a puppy food that meets all of the requirements for his health and growth. The same applies for the mature coonhound. In Chapter 13, I will discuss the diet of your Treeing Walker Coonhound in detail.

Watching the Personality Emerge

Treeing Walker Coonhounds are extremely lovable and affectionate. If there was ever a dog who thrived on attention, I believe it is the Treeing Walker Coonhound. These dogs are generally very content hounds.

As a rule, Treeing Walker Coonhounds are not mean or ill-tempered, unless there is an underlying factor such as a serious illness like a brain

Photo Courtesy of
Tia Schmelzer

tumor. Oh, they'll bark and save you from the FedEx delivery person or elementary kid selling wrapping paper, but usually once the barking stops, the intruder will be met with some serious sniffing and tail-wagging.

Whether you are single or have a family, whoever lives in your house with you and your Treeing Walker Coonhound will be adopted into his pack. He will be comfortable around you and everyone who lives with him. Treeing Walker Coonhounds are the consummate Equal Opportunity Employer, giving everyone ample opportunities to love on him, pet him, play with him, and feed him.

In Chapter 9 , you will learn more about these fascinating hound dogs. These dogs are loyal and faithful. I simply cannot imagine my life without a Treeing Walker Coonhound.

Veterinary Care

Your teenage/adult Treeing Walker Coonhound will not need as many series of vaccinations as he did when he was a puppy. He will need a Bordatella vaccination every six months, especially if he is boarded or gets to go to doggy day care or the dog park. Other than that, adult coonhounds will only need annual vaccinations for rabies and DHPP. Your veterinarian may recommend vaccinating your Treeing Walker Coonhound every year or every other year for Coronavirus, Leptospirosis, Lyme Disease, and influenza.

The veterinarian can also check your coonhound's blood titer for the presence of the vaccinations, which could prevent you from having to get vaccinations every year. Blood titer tests are expensive, so you will need to weigh the cost of them versus annual vaccinations. You will also need to see what your local or state ordinance is regarding the rabies vaccination. It could be required every year or every three years.

Once your Treeing Walker Coonhound is one year old, he will need to be checked for the presence of heart worms, especially if he lives near a water source. If he has been on a heart worm preventative, he should be free from heart worms but it is still a good idea to have him checked annually. Monthly heartworm treatments are available from your veterinarian or they can be shipped to your house each month. There are oral chews or liquid doses that are rubbed between the shoulder blades. Check with your veterinarian and see if the heart worm preventatives also work for other parasites. Many of them do, which will alleviate worming your coonhound every three months.

Barring any unfortunate accidents or illnesses, your Treeing Walker Coonhound will require very little veterinary care, except for annual vaccinations.

CHAPTER 7

Training Your Treeing Walker Coonhound

As I've mentioned, Treeing Walker Coonhounds are very intelligent dogs. Training them generally should not be much of a problem. There are countless books (Lucky Dog Lessons is an excellent book) and internet resources regarding training your coonhound. If you do not feel comfortable tackling the training by yourself, employ a professional dog trainer to help you and your Treeing Walker Coonhound. Chances are that your coonhound will enjoy the training session and challenges that they bring.

Select a Reliable Trainer

Photo Courtesy of Tia Schmelzer

When and if you decide to take your Treeing Walker Coonhound to get trained, research the dog trainer just as you researched the breeder from whom you got your coonhound. Ask your friends who they used. Check with your veterinarian for recommendations. Perhaps your breeder knows a trainer and if your breeder showed coonhounds, they might even be trainers themselves. If they are nearby, you might employ their knowledge, especially since they are familiar with Treeing Walker Coonhounds. You can also check with rescue organizations regarding their experiences with, and recommendations for, a reliable and competent dog trainer.

Your coonhound's safety and well-being should be first and foremost when selecting a trainer. Reputations, whether good or bad, may precede the dog trainer. This is why recommendations are crucial.

Chances are, if the trainer has been established for years, he or she is reputable and knowledgeable. Ask if you can come and observe a class to see how the trainer actually reacts with the dogs.

Your Treeing Walker Coonhound will most likely enjoy being around other dogs in a class and the extra socialization will be good for him. You will also learn by watching other people with their dogs. Perhaps their dog needs a little encouragement or extra attention from the trainer for a particular problem. This is a good time to pay attention because I guarantee you will learn some nuggets of information, even if it might not apply to your coonhound now or ever.

Class sizes are usually limited to a certain number of dogs, say around five to ten dogs, so the trainer won't have a whole bunch of dogs to train and observe at once. Each class should be structured so that one command and cue is learned at a time. Since you will be learning as much as your Treeing Walker Coonhound is learning, you will be able to practice through the week (homework) in order to reinforce the training until your next session.

You might also check and see if the trainer you are interested in will give you private instruction at your house. You will have to pay more, but it might be easier than you taking your hound to a dog training class, at least for a lesson or two.

Obedience Training

Basic obedience training is very important on several levels: for your coonhound's safety, focus, attention, to expand his intelligence, and for your peace of mind. You will want your coonhound to know the very basics, such as sit, lay down, stay, recall, walking on a leash, and not jumping on people.

You can research various training methods and work on your own, or you can employ a trainer and attend training classes. During a basic obedience session, which usually lasts about six weeks, your coonhound will learn simple and basic commands like sit, stay, lay down, heel, and recall. If you wish to expand the training for your coonhound, the dog trainer should have more intense classes, courses and workshops. Investing in a good harness will be helpful for your Treeing Walker Coonhound if he pulls against his collar, or doesn't know how to walk on a leash, whether you are training him yourself or using a professional dog trainer.

Remember that patience, persistence, and practice will allow your coonhound to learn what you are asking him to do. When you begin your training sessions, you want to remove as many distractions as possible. So if your coonhound is excited about going for a walk, it probably isn't a great time to work on something. It is, however, a good time to practice what he may have already learned. Bowie has to sit while I snap on his harness as well as sit by the door before we go out for his walk. Otherwise it's like the starting bell at the Kentucky Derby. During our walks, I will have him stop and sit. I might tell Bowie to "stay" and lengthen the leash. Then I will call him to me. When we resume our walk, I tell Bowie to "heel."

Additionally, training can be accomplished during brief moments when it doesn't feel like a training session. You might be watching television and your Treeing Walker Coonhound has determined that he needs to be in your lap or next to you. This is a great and relaxing opportunity to incorporate "sit" or "down" without your coonhound realizing that he is in school.

Photo Courtesy of
Sara Spies Karotkin

Simple Training Methods

Should you decide to train your coonhound yourself, there are a few commands that are fairly simple to teach to your hound. You can begin incorporating training sessions with your coonhound puppy, too, even if he doesn't yet walk on a leash. Keep your training sessions short. Ten to fifteen minutes, maybe twice a day, is enough. You don't want your coonhound to get bored or resentful. Keep it fun. Short and sweet.

You may or may not decide to use treats as a reward for your coonhound when he does what you ask. Some dogs are treat-motivated, others are toy-motivated. Determine which type of motivation your hound enjoys and go with that. If it is a treat, break his treats into small pieces and reward him as he accomplishes his task. You will want to make sure that the training sessions occur when your coonhound is hungry, making him a little more motivated. Note that Treeing Walker Coonhounds are almost always hungry, so your training session should occur before mealtime.

The problem I see with treat rewards is that your scent hound will smell your stash of treats in your hand or pocket, or he will hear the bag crackle, and that will be his focus. You can get his attention by holding his favorite treat (any treat is a favorite of Bowie's) out in front of him to get his attention. After he completes what is asked of him, you may give him a bite of treat. If he is toy-motivated, show him his toy to get him focused and then let him play with his toy a few minutes when he completes his tasks.

He will catch on quickly that he will be rewarded when he does what is asked of him. As your training progresses, you can cut down on the treats and play time by asking him a few times to perform his task, then reward him. Otherwise, he may expect a treat every time he sits or lays down! Always begin and end your training sessions with a treat or toy, keeping the mood positive and fun.

While I am not a professional dog trainer by any means, I did glean some training tips from Casey's K9 University training. And, as noted above, I read an excellent book, Lucky Dog Lessons by Brandon McMillan, who is a professional dog and animal trainer in Hollywood. This book is easy to read and simple to follow. I highly recommend it.

We will discuss using words for different commands a bit later; you might want to use different words or even a foreign language or hand signal. However, for simplicity's sake, in these next few steps, I am using "sit," "down," "stay," "come," and "off." Remember that you don't need to yell the commands. That will incorporate negativity and possibly fear. Use a calm voice while saying the words firmly. When you are teaching your coonhound to recall, or to come to you, make your voice friendlier and happier, encouraging him to come to you.

- **SIT**

Probably the most common method of teaching a dog to sit on command is to press down on his hindquarters while saying "sit." I would say your dog's name first to get his attention. "Bowie. Sit." Make sure that you aren't shoving your dog down as he will start to associate possible pain or a harsh touch with this training method. You want to be firm, but also gentle. I don't recommend yelling "SIT!" either as that will connote negativity and possibly induce fear. Additionally, if your dog doesn't understand what you want, he might think that you're angry at him and he could resent that since he hasn't done anything wrong. More than likely, your dog isn't deaf and he will hear you the first time you tell him to sit. As your coonhound's education persists, you will be able to barely tap him on his hindquarters when you say "sit" and then your training will progress to a point to where your coonhound will sit when you tell him to sit.

Another method to incorporate "sit" is to attach a leash to your coonhound's collar. A harness will not work well as you will be pulling his back upwards. With a firm, but not too firm, and also gentle hand, begin to pull up on the leash. Say his name and tell him to sit as you are gently pulling up on the leash. You aren't trying to stretch his neck out like a giraffe. Your coonhound will move his hindquarters in the opposite direction, thereby sitting. Be sure you praise him and pet him. Give him a treat.

Your hound may not sit immediately. If he doesn't sit within ten seconds or so, release the leash, wait a little bit, and try it again, telling him to "sit" as you gently pull up on the leash. When he sits, be sure you praise and pet him and tell him "Good Sit!" Dogs like to hear you tell them that they are a good boy or a good girl! Repeating the word for the command you are teaching him reinforces that word to your coonhound, too.

As I mentioned, your dog is probably not deaf. (If he is, incorporate sign language.) If he doesn't sit as soon as you tell him to, don't get mad or impatient or discouraged, especially if this is his first lesson. Even if he's had a few lessons, he might not immediately sit. But he did hear you so give him some time to sit. You might have to repeat yourself a little, but he will get the idea. Give him some praise, and a treat or toy, when he sits.

- **DOWN**

Cuing your coonhound to lay down, on his belly like a sphinx rather than on his side like it's nap time, is also a good segue from the sitting position. Snap on his leash. Say your hound's name to get his attention, then "down." As you tell him "down," pull down gently, but firmly, on the leash. If

Photo Courtesy of
Ann Jayne

he doesn't immediately go down, just wait, holding the leash down. He might resist at first, but he will get it and lie down. Praise him.

Another way is to take your coonhound's front paws and start to walk them away from him as you tell him "down." This might take some time, as well. Nothing should ever be rushed. If you or your coonhound start to get frustrated, take a break. *Always* end your training session on a positive and happy note.

If you have rescued a coonhound, something as simple as "down" might present a problem. Casey was very good with all of his cues except "down." He simply would not lie down when I said "down." I believe it was because he had probably been beaten and most assuredly screamed at. Lying down was a vulnerable position for him. My trainer observed Casey resisting. I told her his story and she told me not to worry about it. It wasn't the end of the world and his comfort and well-being and trust of me were more important. So we never worked on "down" again and Casey still graduated from K9 University!

● **STAY**

Teaching your coonhound to stay can go hand-in-hand, or hand-in-paw, with teaching him to sit or lay down. You don't want to overload him with new commands constantly, so make sure he's progressed fairly well with "sit" and "down."

Once mastered, "stay" might save your hound's life should he break away from you and run towards a street. Telling him to "stay" can prevent him from getting hit by a car or running into any other dangerous scenarios.

Snap his leash on his collar or harness. Make sure he has already had his walk or else he will think he's going on a walk, get super-excited, and you can kiss your training session and his focus good-bye for a while.

Tell him to "stay" and take a step away from him. Maybe use a hand signal, too. If he gets up, tell him to sit or lay down again. Repeat this process again. I would start the training for "stay" by only taking one step, maybe two, away from your coonhound, until the idea cements itself into his brain. Give him some praise, maybe a bit of treat, and tell him "Good!" Don't get too excited with your voice, even if you are excited. It will get your coonhound fired up and he may lose focus. Stay calm.

As he learns to stay, you can take more steps away from him, getting to the end of the leash. As your coonhound graduates from the end of the leash, take him into your backyard and take off the leash. Then you can practice and teach him to stay as you get farther away from him. It is important to do this in an enclosed yard or even your house. I don't recommend taking him off-leash where he can sprint off.

This is a good time to work on recall, calling him to you. Whether you are one step away, one length of the leash away, or across your yard, when you call his name and tell him to come to you, maybe even patting your thigh, he will be happy to walk or run over to you.

Photo Courtesy of
Julia Bland

● COME

Having your coonhound come to you (recall) when you ask him to is a very important command. Like "stay," it could possibly save his life if there is danger around, such as a venomous snake or sharp drop-off. It is important for your Treeing Walker Coonhound to learn recall so he knows that being by your side is a safe place to be.

Without knowing it, telling your hound to come to you will probably begin in the puppy stage if you have a puppy. Your coonhound will need to get used to his name, so you might as well say his name and then add "come" in a happy voice, maybe even patting your side. Tell him "Good Come!" when he obeys.

However, should you adopt an older coonhound, or begin your training after the puppy stage, it's not too late. It is really never to late to teach your dog commands. It may take a little longer, but realistically, training never stops.

"Come" might be easier to learn after your coonhound has mastered "stay." It will almost be like a reward for him. And you as well.

Teaching the recall goes hand-in-hand with "stay." But you can also practice it when your coonhound is on the other side of the room or yard, calling his name and saying, "Come!"

But to begin, you will need to start with your hound only a few feet away. Say his name to get his attention. Show him a treat or toy then say, "Come." When he comes over to you, praise him and give him a bite of treat or let him chew on his toy. If he knows you have a bag of treats, he will probably follow you. This is where "stay" will come in really handy.

You might even have your coonhound on a leash and as you step away, make sure he stays. If he is busy sniffing something, take this opportunity to step to the end of the leash. Get his attention by calling his name, and then say, "Come." Praise and reward him.

To keep your coonhound safe, train him to come to you in your house or your fenced yard. You can even go into another room and call him to you, or the other side of the yard. Make it fun for him. If you ask him to come to you from another room, make it worth his while and give him a treat.

Once your coonhound obeys you, you might even have him sit or lay down, reinforcing those commands as well.

● OFF

Treeing Walker Coonhounds are considered a large breed of dog. They tree raccoons and in this process, stand on their hind legs with their forelegs on the tree. You have the potential to be a human tree. But if your coonhound jumps up on someone, especially someone smaller or old, he could unintentionally hurt them. Teaching your coonhound not to jump on people is a very important part of his education.

It's very common to yell "DOWN!" if your dog jumps up on you or anyone else. As we will discuss in the next section, it is important to use different words for different commands.

I think the easiest way to teach a dog not to jump up on

FUN FACT
2019 PKC World Champion

A Treeing Walker Coonhound named "Bank" took home the grand prize at the Professional Kennel Club (PKC) World Championship in October 2019. The then- three-year-old pup, whose full name is WCH PCH GR NITE CH CH 'PR' Money in the Bank, beat 800 Coonhounds for the title and took home $30,000 in winnings with his co-owner handler Kevin Cable, Jr. Previously, Bank won at the Earl Floyd Ford Pro Classic in Kentucky. Shortly after winning the PKC title, he also won all three nights at the Pro Classic in Indiana.

you or anyone else is to lift up your knee as he jumps up and say "OFF!" firmly. Again, you don't have to yell or scream, but say "OFF!" firmly as jumping up on people is not acceptable behavior. The knee gets in his way and that isn't any fun. If he's running exuberantly towards you, then running into a human knee might smart a little bit. I know some people who thrust their knee into their dogs' chests to teach them to not jump up on them. I see no need for that, especially if you're a large human. You don't want to hurt your hound. It's also a good way to lose your balance.

Simply lifting my knee up and saying "OFF!" when Casey jumped up on me worked like a charm. He figured it out after about three times. Bowie has never really jumped up on me but if he does, I will simply lift up my knee and tell him "OFF."

If you have problems with your balance, or perhaps knee issues, you can also teach your coonhound not to jump up on you by simply turning your back to him when he jumps up. He won't get petted and he won't get to see your face. Be sure and say "OFF!" in a stern voice, without yelling, as you turn your back to him. When he gets back on all fours, praise him and reward him.

Use Your Words

Even though Casey took an obedience course at K9 University in Oklahoma City, Oklahoma, the owner and main dog trainer, Angel, also made a couple of house calls to help Casey. One of the most useful nuggets I took away from having Angel help Casey was how important it is to use different words for different commands.

Most everyone says "sit" when they want their dog to sit. As was previously noted, "down" is common to say when you want your coonhound to lay down. However, when your hound jumps up on you, what do you say? Probably "DOWN!" Does your Treeing Walker Coonhound immediately lie down? Maybe, but I doubt it. If he does, well, congratulations are in order. At that moment, you simply want the hound to get off of you, not necessarily lie down. If you train your coonhound with "down" in order to lie down, then it will be confusing to tell him "down" if he jumps up on you. However, you still need another word. As discussed, I use "OFF!" but you can choose whatever word in whatever language you want.

Suffice it to say that we end up mixing our words, the same words, for different actions. And our old friend "No" is used for everything.

Rummaging through the trash..."NO!"

Getting on the furniture..."NO!" (With the exception of our bed, Bowie and Ajax are never told "No" regarding being on the sofa or living room chairs or the other beds in the house.)

Jumping up on someone..."NO!"

Barking..."NO!"

Get the idea? Your coonhound is told "NO" for almost everything he does. So as the ones "in charge," we need to be consistent with choosing different words that are specific for different actions.

Casey had a territorial issue after we rescued him. His yard and his house were *his*. So while I appreciate Casey's protection, it had to have limits. We have pool-cleaning men and landscapers who come to the yard once/week. They have to get in the backyard, which was Casey's backyard. So we called Angel to come out and help us.

To Casey, Angel was a stranger in his yard. So Casey barked and growled and followed Angel around. Angel told us to select a word, *one specific word,* for Casey to understand that this was not acceptable behavior and that he needed to stop it.

We selected "Halt!" because, like "No," the word "Stop" is used frequently for different things. Confusion is not the goal. Obedience is.

Casey was on a leash and as he began barking at Angel, David or I would yell "Halt!" and tug on the leash. It only took a few times before Casey got it. Then we tried it without the leash and as one of us said "Halt," Casey stopped and went in the dog house. He fretted a little bit but then settled down. "Halt!" was also used when someone appeared at the front door to Casey's domain.

Another thing regarding words that I hadn't considered, but it makes perfect sense, is to choose words that do not sound like other words. My friend, Courtney, learned this with the training classes she took with her German Shepherds, George and Ralph.

When you are teaching your Treeing Walker Coonhound to walk on a leash and walk calmly beside you, the most common term is "Heel." But, when you are wanting to get your hound to come to you, "Here" might be the most common word of choice. As Courtney's trainer informed her, "Heel" and "Here" are similar sounding words. So she gave Courtney a German word, "Foos" to use instead of "Here." (FYI horses are very attuned to "Whoa," so any long O sounding word might cause your steed to stop.)

Think of things that you would like your coonhound to learn and come up with different words for the cues. If you happen to be fluent in another language, you can use foreign words. Write the words down, for your benefit as well as anyone who might take care of your coonhound for you. If you use foreign words, be sure and write the pronunciation for people who will care for your coonhound but aren't fluent in the foreign language you used.

Here are some commands you will want to teach your coonhound, so discover words that you want to use to convey to your hound.

- Sit
- Stay
- Lie down
- Walking on a leash
- Calling your dog to you (recall)
- Not jumping on you, other people, or other things
- Stop barking
- Drop something, like your shoe or favorite blanket
- Other actions

If you have a Treeing Walker Coonhound puppy, begin teaching him these words for the specific actions. As you say the words, gently press your hands on his rear end to get him to sit or, from a seated position, gently pull his forelegs down to get him to lie down. And even though he's a puppy and gets excited and jumps up on you and it's really cute and heart-warming, begin to tell him "Off" and place his front paws back on the floor. By the time he is a year or two older, he should respond quickly and appropriately to the word cues.

Different sounds work, too. Bowie unselfishly tried to help me eat my donuts so I gave him the "time's up" buzzer sound. How do I write it? I don't know.

"EEEHHHNNNKKK!"

Make up your own buzzer sound and apply it to your coonhound when he sticks his nose into your donuts.

After your Treeing Walker Coonhound has successfully completed the requested task, be sure that you use his name and praise him. Pet him, too. Treats can be used but your coonhound will figure that little reward out quickly! Save a treat for the end of the training session, walk, or event. You may not always have treats with you, but you always have kind words with you.

Barking

Remember that your Treeing Walker Coonhound is a hunting dog. Part of his job is to alert his owner and whoever else is around that there is a raccoon in the tree. He does that by barking. That is part of his nature. While coonhounds don't bark constantly, they do bark. Keep that in mind.

When you are training your coonhound to hold it down a notch or two, or even stop barking, you can come up with a word to try and get your coonhound to stop barking. "Halt" is a good one. So is "Hush." Maybe use "Quiet" rather than yelling "SHUT UP!"

I also use a vibrating collar for Bowie when he is in the yard and I'm gone. He has one particular area of the yard that we have designated the Bark Zone and for whatever reason(s), he has worn a trail in that area, barking his head off. Deer pass by this area and we have lots of trees, so there could be a squirrel nest in the trees or raccoons. It could be that critters ramble through this area at night trying to get to the bird feeder. If we lived in the country, I wouldn't care. But I don't think our neighbors want to hear Bowie. He doesn't do it all of the time; he can be quite content lying on the lounger. I guess it just depends upon the previous night's activities by the woodland creatures.

The collar beeps and vibrates when Bowie barks. For the most part, he responds to it. However, when he's coming in the house, he barks and knows he gets a treat so the vibration and beeping are a moot point.

Casey didn't like his vibrating collar. He shook his head each time it vibrated and finally decided if he didn't bark, it didn't vibrate. Intelligence.

Treeing Walker Coonhound vocalizations will be discussed further in Chapter 11. These dogs can be very vocal, but they always have a reason.

Crate Training

For me, the jury is still out on using a crate. There are positives and negatives to it. The positives certainly outweigh the negatives, but both need to be addressed.

First and foremost, people need to understand that a crate is not a place of punishment nor should your coonhound be kept inside the crate for extended lengths of time. Dog crates are places where your coonhound can have a little private time and feel safe. He should never feel threatened in his crate or be locked in there for hours on end. That is my biggest problem with using a crate, probably due to my experiences with animal rescue and knowledge of puppy mills. If a coonhound is punished, say for chewing up something or having an indoor accident, placing him in the crate makes him associate the crate with punishment. When you try to get him to go in there while you are vacuuming or taking a bath, he probably won't be very receptive because he will still think you are punishing him for something. The crate will become a jail cell to your coonhound rather than his safe place.

Since the crate is your Treeing Walker Coonhound's personal space, like a dog bed, unless he is a puppy, he probably won't go to the bathroom in the crate. Leaving him locked in there for hours and hours will be excruciating as he won't want to soil his place. There is also the high possibility that he will drink all of his water or perhaps spill it, possibly becoming dehydrated.

If you do decide to *properly* use a crate, make sure that it is large enough to accommodate your Treeing Walker Coonhound. He should be able to lie down, stand up, and turn around comfortably. An extra-large crate should be fine, even when your coonhound is a puppy. Getting your puppy familiar with the extra-large crate will prevent you from having to purchase larger crates if you start with a small one. The extra-large crate will give your puppy room to play and move around as he grows, and will be a familiar and comforting place of rest and refuge for him.

The dog crate should be comfortable, with a nice soft pad or cushion in it and a blanket or two. A few toys can be placed in there as well as a bowl of water and perhaps a few nibbles of food.

While you are at home with your Treeing Walker Coonhound, leave the gate to the crate open. That way, he can go in and out at his will. There won't be the threat of locking him in there.

Training your coonhound to go in the crate should not be terribly diffi-cult. My experience with crate-training a dog was with a Great Dane mix pup. Juliet was a foster dog. I moved the crate into my bedroom so I could let her out in the middle of the night if she needed out.

To get Juliet in the crate, I simply gave her a treat, then put a treat inside the crate. The first couple of nights I had to put her in there. But a few days later, when it was bedtime, she went in by herself. I still gave her a treat and praised her. You might say, "Crate" to get your coonhound used to that command. You won't want to sound like a drill sergeant, but rather use a kind but firm voice. If your coonhound will be spending the night in the crate, you can practice by enticing him in the crate throughout the day to help get him used to it.

Although I have never kept Bowie or Ajax in a crate, they were spell-bound with Juliet's crate. During the day I moved it into the living room and put Juliet in it while I went to work for a couple of hours. I wasn't gone for a long period of time, and I made sure she went outside and used the bath-room before putting her in the crate.

When the crate was in the living room and the door was open, Ajax and Bowie decided it was a quite comfortable place to rest. They would both go in and out of the crate! No negativity was associated with it and I kept the door open for them. I laughed when they went in and lay down.

Socializing Your Treeing Walker Coonhound

Socializing your coonhound is very important. Treeing Walker Coonhounds were bred to hunt in packs. They are, for the most part, natu-rally social. That's not to say that your coonhound will just accept any dog he meets on the street or at the dog park or in doggy day care. If you are the proud owner of a Treeing Walker Coonhound puppy, start his socialization early so he's familiar with meeting dogs. You will want to introduce him to friendly dogs, perhaps other puppies. If you know a dog who is not particu-larly fond of other dogs or who is fiercely protective of his owner, you should keep your coonhound, whether a puppy or adult hound, away from that dog.

Photo Courtesy of
Sandy Addona

If you have other dogs, your Treeing Walker Coonhound should be used to them. Also, if you have taken your coonhound to doggy day care, he will learn how to get along with other dogs, play with them, and have a great time.

Bringing a Treeing Walker Coonhound into your home if you have other dogs, or bringing other dogs into your home to meet/live with your Treeing Walker Coonhound, should be done slowly and with great observation. All dogs can be jealous of other dogs "intruding" on their masters and their territory. Think how you feel when someone who hasn't been invited comes over and disrupts your day. Your coonhound may feel that way too. If your coonhound is the "new guy," he may be a little nervous.

Watch for signs of aggression or fear. Raised hackles and bared teeth are obvious signs of a threatening dog. A severely tucked-in tail can also indicate fear, uncertainty, and discomfort. If your hound feels threatened, he might lash out or bite, even with a tucked-in tail.

If you notice your coonhound's tail is relaxed or curled over his back, he is more alert and attentive and perhaps even ready to make a new friend and play. The down dog position (rear end in the air and forelegs on the ground) indicates that your coonhound is ready to play. Friendly paw-swatting might be observed as well. The ears should be alert, not pinned back or flattened against his head. Your coonhound might even have a happy expression on his face, ready to have a good time with his new friend.

Your Treeing Walker Coonhound's unique nose will be further discussed in Chapter 8. For now, note that part of dogs' socialization involves sniffing each other, particularly sniffing each other's rear ends. Your Treeing Walker Coonhound is learning about the other dog. Is he afraid? Is she in heat? Is he friendly? Have I met her before? Lots of questions are answered by sniffing. Information is logged. Data is recorded. Assessments are made.

While we think it's gross, it can be like our equivalent of shaking hands. If you notice your Treeing Walker Coonhound shy away from having his privates sniffed, or the other dog does, separate the dogs for a bit until they get more used to each other. Not everyone is willing to shake hands, so it should be reasonable that not every dog wants his butt sniffed.

When I brought Casey home for the first time, I put him on a leash so my beagles, Ajax and Lucy, could see him. I took him to the backyard where we have a separate fenced dog pen. Casey didn't want to stay there without me and this was only a few hours after we had met! To make a long story short, it was getting dark and top that off with the sprinklers coming on, I made the executive decision to bring Casey in the house. He did not have a problem with Ajax at all. He really didn't pay him any mind. However, Casey was intact and was very interested in little Lucy, who turned into a wild lioness when he tried some coonhound foreplay with her.

Casey never had problems with other dogs, either. When he went to obedience training, he was quite content to be by my side. At doggy day care (there was also an introductory class), he participated in some group play, but then sometimes he checked himself into an open crate (even though I had never crate trained him). I know this from the report cards he got as well as phone calls from the techs. They called because they were concerned that Casey didn't feel well when he actually just wanted to be left alone. The doggy day care also had a phone app with a camera so I could turn on the app and watch him and Ajax!

Although I am not a dog trainer by any means, I highly suggest that you make sure that your Treeing Walker Coonhound is properly socialized before you ever take him to a dog park. Exercise caution because not everyone there will have made sure that their dog is friendly to strange dogs. I suggest making your coonhound's first dog park exposure one in which the dog park is not very crowded. Then walk him around on a leash for a little bit to see how he acclimates to the dog park. Watch your coonhound's body language and see if he's receptive to running and cavorting, or if he wants to stay by your side. You might even sit with him and observe the other dogs for a while before you decide to let him off leash.

Digging

From my experience, Treeing Walker Coonhounds are not notorious diggers. The only digging Casey ever did was underneath the bushes by my bedroom or spruce tree. He made a little cool nest where he could hide, nap, or take his rawhides and enjoy them.

Bowie seems to enjoy digging. While our yard doesn't resemble the Grand Canyon, he does have a few select places where he enjoys digging. One in particular is the area where I have attempted to make a flower garden that will rival anything in a magazine. Hint: I'm not there yet. Not even close. For some reason, maybe due to the sprinkler and the dirt being soft, Bowie has dug a small crater. He has a blast, too. I have pretty much resigned this spot to Bowie. I even play with him in this spot and say, "Dig, dig, dig!" He obliges me, slinging dirt everywhere. I simply sweep the dirt back into the hole. Bowie will bark at me and I'll bark at him and we have a great time. If he tries to dig somewhere else in my attempted garden, he gets the buzzer sound. To date, I still have not found a magazine photograph of a beautiful garden with a Treeing Walker Coonhound hole excavated among the flowers.

A couple of other places are in a flower bed that the people who lived here had made. (They also planted holly everywhere and I'm in the process of removing it as I can.) It has shrubs (which I plan to remove) in it and a large rock where I will sit and watch Bowie and Ajax dig to their hearts' content. They will move from one place to the other. These are the only places where they are allowed to dig and they know it.

One tip from K9 University to keep your dog from digging is this: put his poop in the hole and cover it up. When the dog digs and finds a cache of dog poop, he will probably get discouraged. But as the trainer noted, if your dog likes to eat poop, this will be a hidden smorgasbord for him! As an alternative, you can sprinkle hot pepper in the hole to discourage digging.

Counter-Surfing/Begging

As noted in Chapter 1, Treeing Walker Coonhounds stand about 25-27 inches on all four legs. When they stand on their hind legs, they almost double in height. Their paws could easily reach the chest, and maybe the shoulders, of a human who is five-and-a-half or six feet tall.

Reaching your countertops will not be difficult for a rearing coonhound. Any food items left close to the edge will be swiped and eaten. This is called counter-surfing. Even standing on all fours, by stretching his neck, your Treeing Walker Coonhound could possibly reach the edge of the counter with his nose, sniffing the area for food left dangerously close to the edge.

Since your coonhound can rear up on a tree, and hop with his back legs when a raccoon is treed, he can do the same with your countertops, thereby being rewarded with the goodies stored there. Your coonhound might not stop there; rather he might walk the length of the counter or island on his hind legs, sniffing and grabbing and licking, searching for sustenance.

So, for starters, keep all of your food that is on the counter at the back of the counter. If you have a kitchen island, keep the food in the middle of the island. Make this a habit as you will not always have eyes on your kitchen. But someone else might. This rule applies to items on your stovetop, too. Besides losing your supper, your coonhound could get burned if he pulls off a hot pan. Don't leave food on the stove unattended, for your sake and your hound's.

If your coonhound happens to counter-surf, you will more than likely yell at him. Yell his name and then "Off!" or whatever word you have chosen for your hound to resume all fours. I realize in circumstances like this, other words might be in your vocabulary, but you shouldn't teach those words to your Treeing Walker Coonhound.

Begging will be discussed further in Chapter 9. Even if you keep your Treeing Walker Coonhound outside while you eat, at some point you will be eating something while he is nearby. He will be extremely interested. If you have no intention of sharing your meal or snack, let him know that he needs to stop begging. You might develop a hand signal, a word, or a sharp clap of your hands to indicate that this is not acceptable behavior. Cuing your coonhound to not beg will be useful when you have dinner guests. Your Treeing Walker Coonhound will work the room, believe me. So let him know that this isn't allowed, either by a verbal or visual command, or by putting him outside.

Leash Training

Leash training can begin when your Treeing Walker Coonhound is a puppy. Under your supervision, you can attach a leash to his collar and let him start dragging it around to get used to it. Then you can start holding the leash and walk your puppy around the house or the yard. Short walks in the neighborhood are fine, too. Remember that your puppy won't be able to take really long walks, so be prepared to carry him if you extend the time of your walk.

Treeing Walker Coonhounds are strong and they might have a tendency to pull. If you are fond of your shoulders staying in their sockets, invest in a sturdy harness or a pronged training collar to be used for walks. Without inflicting pain, but bringing awareness to the hound, the pronged collar will help alleviate any pulling. He needs to listen to you and learn to heel, so a gentle tug with the leash attached to the pronged collar will refocus him.

As you begin to use a leash, be consistent with your Treeing Walker Coonhound. If you prefer having him on your left side, stay with that. Same thing if you prefer him on your right side. When you begin to walk, say, "Heel," or "Name of your dog, Heel," then lead with your opposite foot. As he starts walking with you, reward him with praise. The goal, besides not pulling on you, is to have your coonhound walking comfortably at your side. At first, you will probably keep your coonhound close to you, on the proverbial short leash. As your leash training progresses, you can lengthen the leash and loosen your grip on it. Eventually your leash may be fairly loose with lots of slack.

Note that you are walking a scent hound, so everything you see on your walk will need to be sniffed. This is fine if time allows. However, if you are still in the training stages, your coonhound needs to know that this is not playtime and that he has business to conduct and lessons to learn. A slight tug on the leash and collar will bring his mind back to the task at hand. At the end of your walk, give him a reward by letting him smell some things.

While you are walking your hound, you might employ some other voice commands, too. Stop periodically, telling your hound to "Stop," "Halt," or whatever word you select. This is also a good time to work on "Stay," so you might tell your coonhound to "Stay," and then loosen the leash until you are the whole leash length away from your Treeing Walker Coonhound. If he walks toward you without you calling him, or follows you, repeat the command. Once he waits for you to call him, give him some praise and pats.

With Casey, I found it easier to work on these exercises, with the exception of "Heel," during the middle or end of our walks. Casey was always excited to go on his walks so his energy level was a little higher and he wasn't as receptive to training. The same thing goes with Bowie. Let your coonhound have some time for excitement about going on the walk, then you can start his education. Treeing Walker Coonhounds enjoy their walks very much.

Off-Leash Training

I have seen many photos of people hiking up mountain trails or at the beach with their coonhounds running off leash. They are beautiful sights. Perhaps wide-open spaces like this are fine for taking your Treeing Walker Coonhound off leash. Perhaps they are not if your hound is not properly trained to come to you when you call.

Before you even think about attempting this, your coonhound must be exceptional at recall. Although they aren't a match for the speed of a greyhound, a very fit and healthy Treeing Walker Coonhound is extremely fast; much faster than you are. If you enjoy the beauty of watching your coonhound run freely, that enjoyment might fade quickly when he doesn't come back when you call and you get to then chase him.

I do not recommend letting your coonhound off-leash at all if you are taking walks in your neighborhood or public parks. Even if the hound is well-trained in recall, excitement can lead to inattention, which could result in running out in front of a car. People in the park might be concerned about a large hound running around, as well. Keep your coonhound's safety in mind at all times and keep him on a leash in public areas.

Even if your Treeing Walker Coonhound is well-behaved when he is off-leash, or even when he is leashed, be aware of any other dogs who are off-leash. They might be aggressive and I know people who have had their coonhounds attacked by off-leash dogs. Always be aware of what is going on around you and your coonhound and if you have a suspicion of another dog, it is best to leash your coonhound and find a place that is safer for you and your hound.

Agility

Treeing Walker Coonhounds are very flexible and agile hounds. Due to their hunting nature, they are athletic, fast, tough, and at times, fearless. As I noted in Chapter 1, Treeing Walker Coonhounds can "climb" up trees or over fences.

Their agility extends to being able to hop up in the air and spin in a circle, sometimes while they are at a standstill. I have witnessed Casey and Bowie do this numerous times. Sometimes they simply spin in circles when they are happy or excited. Treeing Walker Coonhounds are adept at hopping backwards on their hind legs. They can easily hop onto your furniture, whether they have been invited or not.

Taking a nap may involve curling into a tiny, tucked up ball referred to as a "coonie curl." Other positions in naps may involve the back legs extended up around the face while the front legs extend to the back legs. A hind leg stretched forward so the hind foot meets or enters the mouth is also a particular flexibility employed by coonhounds. Lying with their heads on the arm of the couch in an almost vertical position is a favorite position, too. These hounds are bred and designed to look up into trees, so what looks terribly uncomfortable to us is quite restful and pleasing for your Treeing Walker Coonhound.

Treeing Walker Coonhounds are never boring. Even while they are asleep. Be sure and take some photos!

CHAPTER 8
Now You Have a Scent Hound

I sometimes wish that God would grant me a day to run as fast as a horse and have the nose of a scent hound. I've read articles about what these dogs can smell and it is astounding. Your Treeing Walker Coonhound is a scent hound, as are beagles, Basset hounds, other coonhound breeds, dachshunds, and bloodhounds.

When you see a car driving by and there is a dog with his head out the window, you probably notice how much he is enjoying the wind in his face. But have you ever stopped to think about how much this dog can smell what is going on around him?

Photo Courtesy of
Lisa Morgan

The Marvelous Nose

There are about five million scent receptors in the human nose. A beagle has 225 million scent receptors and a bloodhound has 300 million. Bloodhounds are the president of the canine sniffing club. Your Treeing Walker Coonhound has about as many scent receptors as a beagle; enough to get the job done.

These smells have to be analyzed, too. The percentage of a dog's brain used to analyze scents and smells is about 40% larger than a human's. Your Treeing Walker Coonhound can smell *at least* 10,000 times better than you can. So when you are going for your evening stroll and your coonhound seems to be smelling nothing but grass, rest assured there is more that he is smelling. Much more.

> **FUN FACT**
> **Professional Kennel Club LLC (PKC)**
>
> The Professional Kennel Club LLC (PKC) is dedicated to the sport of competitive raccoon hunting and is the largest organization devoted to the registration of Coonhounds. Headquartered in Evansville, Indiana, the PKC sponsors several annual competitions, including a World Championship, a National Championship, and a Futurity Championship. PKC events do not permit the use of firearms, and no game is taken during their events. The PKC also licenses over 8,000 night hunts for Coonhounds annually. For more information about this club, visit www.prohound.com.

Humans inhale and exhale through the same air passages. Smells go in one way and they go out the same way. When we smell bread, our brain tells us that it is bread, maybe that it is a little stale or too yeasty. Your Treeing Walker Coonhound's brain can tell you things like what type of grain was used in the flour (perhaps even the brand of flour that you used), the yeast, the non-stick spray for the pan, how old the bread is, and your scent that is lingering in the bread. (Eating the bread probably doesn't require your Treeing Walker Coonhound to use as much math or information gathering.)

When your Treeing Walker Coonhound smells something, he uses two different air passages. One air passage is for smelling and one is for breathing. He can store the smell in his nose while he is exhaling. If that isn't enough, your coonhound can wiggle each nostril independently of the other one. That's cute. It also means that your coonhound can inhale smells separately in each nostril, independent from the other nostril, and then determine what smell came from what nostril! So when you are taking your Treeing Walker Coonhound for a walk and he might be weaving left and right, it's because he's smelling something from his left nostril and then

Photo Courtesy of Amanda Brimmer

the right nostril. Maybe your coonhound smelled a deer scent out of his left nostril and a raccoon scent out of his right nostril. He will more than likely veer to the right to find that rascally raccoon.

Take some time and study your Treeing Walker Coonhound's nose. Get a good look at it while your hound is snoozing on your lap or perhaps sniffing something. When your coonhound has his wet nose in your face, know that his nose helps trap scents and particles. Things stick to a wet nose.

Your Treeing Walker Coonhound has his very own unique nose print, too, just like a paw print or a finger print. There are companies who register the nose prints in a database to help locate lost or stolen dogs.

Once a smell is inhaled, it can remain in the nose, perhaps pushed even deeper for processing, or it can be pushed out through the sides of the nose. As your coonhound is sniffing, air that is already in the nose can be displaced. While you are studying your Treeing Walker Coonhound's nose, notice the little curly cue slits on the sides of his nose. Air that is already in the nose, as well as scents, is pushed out and back through these slits. But as this is done, these air and scent particles also create a small air current that helps your coonhound inhale more new scents. Sniffing has just taken on a whole new meaning. Sniffing has gotten real.

What Treeing Walker Coonhounds Can Smell

What your Treeing Walker Coonhound can smell can probably be summed up with one simple question. What can't they smell?

Remember that your coonhound has 225,000,000 scent receptors in his nose. Those scent receptors allow your coonhound to smell the equivalent of a teaspoon of sugar in one million gallons of water! That is not one, but two, Olympic-sized swimming pools. Equate this marvelous sense of smell to vision and it is akin to your Treeing Walker Coonhound clearly seeing something that is 3,000 miles away! So Bowie, who lives in Oklahoma, could see a steak dinner in California.

When you are taking your Treeing Walker Coonhound on a walk and he starts to sniff, he is smelling the grass and the dirt and the deer who left a hoofprint in the dirt. He can also smell other dogs who walked by with their owners, smell their owners, and can tell from scents from the foot pads or urine if the dog was agitated, happy, or in heat. Your Treeing Walker Coonhound can smell the leaf on the ground, the decay of the leaf, each fold of the leaf, a caterpillar who chewed on the leaf, and raindrops on the leaf. If you stuck your nose down to the ground, you would smell the leaf and maybe the dirt, possibly without being able to make any distinction between the two.

Dogs, and other animals including reptiles, have a remarkable organ in their noses called the vomeronasal organ, also known as Jacobsen's organ. Your Treeing Walker Coonhound's vomeronasal organ is a small bone above the hard palate at the floor of the nasal septum. It houses the sensory cells and receptor sites, which carry the molecules of whatever is being smelled on tiny cilia (hairs). The function of this organ is to detect chemicals found in pheromones, allowing your coonhound to determine if another coonhound is ready for mating. It also allows a newborn Treeing Walker Coonhound puppy to find his mother's milk and distinguish his mother from other nursing mamas.

Along with a coonhound's life necessities such as food and sex, your Treeing Walker Coonhound's vomeronasal organ will allow him to determine human emotions such as fear, anxiety, anger, and sadness. Humans can emit smells and stink, either through body odor, sweat, bodily fluids, and tears. So the old adage that "dogs can smell fear," is actually quite true. Fear can release adrenalin, sweat, and an increase in blood flow and heart rate.

As if the coonhound nose isn't marvelous enough, your Treeing Walker Coonhound might be able to detect diseases, including cancer. If your coonhound is paying special attention to one part of your body, say a mole on your arm, this could be a warning sign. Don't panic, but be sure that you get a second opinion from a human doctor. Dogs have been known to alert their owners to the presence of various forms of cancer, as well as oncoming seizures and glucose levels in diabetics.

Everything Gets Sniffed

Sniffing will be second-nature to your Treeing Walker Coonhound. Things around your house, in your yard, at your vet's office, in your car, and on your walks, will get a thorough going-over.

But it doesn't stop there. You and your friends and family will not be immune from the Treeing Walker Coonhound nose. Yes, he recognizes your scent. But when you come home and you're happy to see him, or you've had a crappy day, he's going to pick up on that. He will also note if you had a hamburger for lunch, walked through some flowers, or cheated on him by petting another dog.

Just in case you are seeing the "other dog" on more than one occasion, your Treeing Walker Coonhound can file away this information in his scent memory. So maybe the next time he won't be as indignant when he discovers

Photo Courtesy of
Alexandra Fabela

Photo Courtesy of
Kevin Thibault

the other dog scent on your pants. He will also recognize this dog's scent if he ever meets him face-to-face. Or face-to-butt. If the dog happens to be a long-lost friend or playmate, your coonhound will recognize this scent that belongs to his friend.

The same thing goes with your friends and family. A well-placed coonhound snout in an inappropriate place on your friend will provide your hound with a ton of information. If your friend is a dog-lover, your coonhound will know this. If your friend happens to be a jerk, your coonhound will know this too and it may be time to get a new friend.

Scent Trails

Treeing Walker Coonhounds can be good for cold and hot trails. Hot trails are fresh scents, maybe a few minutes or a few hours old. A cold trail can be from scents laid down the previous day or several days ago. I can always tell when some sort of critter has scurried around on my patio during the night because Bowie and Ajax go nuts smelling and bawling and baying.

If you want to give your Treeing Walker Coonhound some additional activities, make a scent trail with something that your hound may be fond of, may not be familiar with, or gets him super-excited. You can drag the item around your yard, making patterns, running it over tree trunks and rocks. Let your coonhound get a whiff of whatever it is and then turn him loose, watching him go to work. Note if he finds the places where you left the scent trail, such as on the tree trunks.

To Hunt or Not to Hunt

Whether or not you decide to take your Treeing Walker Coonhound on raccoon hunts, keep in mind that you still have a hunting dog. Your coonhound will be "on the hunt" when you take him for walks. He's going to smell what ran through the walking trail or across the street five minutes ago or the day before. Chances are extremely high that he will alert you to the scent he found by baying, barking or perhaps howling. The Treeing Walker Coonhound Vocal System will be discussed in Chapter 11. Just know that as a hunting dog, alerting the owner to the presence of a treed raccoon is just another day at the office for the Treeing Walker Coonhound.

Although the Treeing Walker Coonhound's cousin, the bloodhound, is probably the world's foremost authority on sniffing and tracking, there's no reason why your coonhound can't "hunt" for other things, such as drugs or missing children.

Hounds employed for this job have their noses saturated with the smell of their "quarry," whether it is an escaped prisoner or a lost child or camper. Even though your coonhound will smell 50 other things, a properly trained tracking hound will disregard all of the many other smells and focus solely on the task at hand. The scent of that child trumps the smells of the deer, rabbits, moldy leaves, pop can, and all other odors that get sucked into the nose of the Treeing Walker Coonhound.

Hounds, including beagles, are excellent for helping police search for illegal narcotics and other drugs. If you see a cute little beagle at the airport sniffing baggage, he's not looking for cookies. Well, he may be, but he is also searching for drugs.

Welcome to the wonderful world of the scent hound. Embrace the Divine Design and enjoy the show.

CHAPTER 9
A Dog Like No Other

Traits and Characteristics

*Photo Courtesy of
Donna Holtzclaw*

Treeing Walker Coonhounds are generally very affectionate and friendly. Even though they are bred to hunt and track, they have a very sweet disposition. Your coonhound will enjoy being around his human pack as well as other dogs in the household. And possibly even cats, although that isn't guaranteed. As you will learn later in this chapter, your Treeing Walker Coonhound will most likely enjoy being as close to you as he can, whether that is enjoying a walk, playing with you, or crawling up in your lap for some petting and snoozing.

We discussed the nose of the Treeing Walker Coonhound fairly extensively in Chapter 8. Since you have a scent hound, your Treeing Walker Coonhound will be curious. Everything will need to be inspected and sniffed. That's just who they are. If you think your coonhound is nosy, well, he is!

Hopelessly Devoted to You

Your Treeing Walker Coonhound will become very devoted to you. These hounds are loyal and it is an honor to become their best friend. Of course, as we discussed, if you rescue a Treeing Walker Coonhound from an abusive situation, there may be some baggage or there may be some hesitancy. However, there may not be. You may be amazed at how well your coonhound will adapt to you, even if he was removed from an abusive situation. These are very forgiving hounds, seeming to forgive

FUN FACT
TWCs in Film

The 1974 film, *Where the Red Fern Grows*, features several Coonhounds, including a pair of Treeing Walker Coonhounds who win the right to compete in a championship along with the main character's dogs. These dogs, owned by the character Mr. Kyle, play a small but critical role in the story. This film is based on a novel of the same name and tells the story of a young boy living in the Ozark Mountains who wants nothing more than a pair of Redbone Coonhounds for hunting.

(and hopefully forget) the atrocities that may have been inflicted on them. As their trust of you grows, they will be devoted and loyal to you since they know that they can trust you. Whether rescued or not, your Treeing Walker Coonhound will appoint himself as your guardian and defender of the home, whether it is from a squirrel, the mailman, FedEx delivery person, or the elementary kid selling wrapping paper.

Casey and Bowie both came from abusive situations. However, Casey, on more than one occasion, put himself between me and perceived danger (the guys who clean our swimming pool as well as a workman we encountered on one of our walks). While Casey was very protective of his home and family, he was as docile as a lamb with his family. Bowie, for all that he has been through, has never met a stranger. He may bark at the Amazon delivery man or he may not. It depends on how much he is enjoying his nap on the couch. Bowie actually smiles when he sleeps.

If you get a puppy or young dog, then he more than likely picked you out, to live with and love for the rest of his life. You will have a very devoted hound for the next 15 years or so. Please don't rule out the devotion that adopting or rescuing or even purchasing an older Treeing Walker Coonhound will have for you. These hounds are just big lovebugs. I think it is just their nature.

Casey enjoyed getting in my lap and being around me, whatever I was doing. Bowie does as well. Part of me knows that they want, and need, attention. Another part of me knows that they simply need to be near me, whether it's on the couch, going for a walk, or lying in the dog bed while I write.

Embrace this devotion.

Photo Courtesy of Keith Bentley

A Loyal Family Member

Treeing Walker Coonhounds adapt readily into their family pack. While your hound may bond with you a little more than with someone else who lives in your household, rest assured that no family member will be deprived of opportunities to love on, pet, snuggle with, or feed, the resident coonhound.

Your Treeing Walker Coonhound will be extremely comfortable around his family. He will think nothing of hopping in your lap and thoughtfully restricting your view of the television or helping you eat whatever it is that you are eating. More than likely, your friends will be his friends and your family will be his family. If you need your bed warmed before you climb into it, chances are your coonhound will be happy to oblige, if he's allowed on the bed. Bowie is not allowed in our bed. It's easy to get a coonhound onto the bed. It's difficult to get him off the bed.

Not only will he be happy to share his life with you, he might even begin to prefer his family over the company of other dogs. That's not to say that your Treeing Walker Coonhound won't want to play with other dogs. He will. But his loyalty will be to you.

Casey always put himself between me and any stranger he perceived as a threat to me. He was a protector, but he was also a very loyal coonhound. That is something you simply can't train a coonhound, or any dog for that matter, to do.

Respect your coonhound and he will respect you. Be loyal to him and he will be loyal. Love him and he will love you until he takes his last breath.

A Hands-On Dog

Unless your coonhound is exploring the yard, chances are there will never be too many hands to pet him. I've watched my son and niece and nephew petting Bowie simultaneously (six hands, 30 fingers). For whatever reason, when one hand was removed, Bowie raised his head and looked at the culprit, and let them know that the hand needs to be placed back on his body where it was. I really don't think that you can pet or love on your Treeing Walker Coonhound enough.

Aside from being a glutton for petting, your coonhound might be a glutton for attention, getting what he wants when he wants it. Never in a mean or malicious way, but rather an endearing and very calculating way. Treeing Walker Coonhounds are persistent and when yours wants a treat, he will inform you through a series of barks, pawing at you, and even standing by the treat jar in case you don't fully grasp what he is telling you.

Easy on the Eyes

Aside from the absolute sweetness that seems to drip from Treeing Walker Coonhounds, they are simply beautiful dogs. Each coat will be distinctively marked and it is fun to look at their markings and admire their beautiful coats. They carry themselves well, whether they are standing still and alert or ambling (or racing) around the yard. When I brought Casey home, I was mesmerized watching him trot around the yard, moving like his feet were on springs, floating off the ground. Treeing Walker Coonhounds are fluid and graceful, even when they are running full-speed ahead with ears flapping behind them, enjoying their lives to the fullest.

Intelligence

I have mentioned several times that Treeing Walker Coonhounds are intelligent. They truly are. In *The Mini-Atlas of Dog Breeds,* Treeing Walker Coonhounds are noted for their intelligence: "These dogs are intelligent and proficient. Training is accomplished with little trouble, as these dogs are able to learn from example."

Although I have never trained a Treeing Walker Coonhound to hunt raccoons or for agility, I truly believe that they can learn easily and by example. I imagine that coonhound pups are trained with experienced coonhounds to tree raccoons, even though it is truly in their nature to tree them. The pups will learn from the older hounds how to stay on target, not veering off for any other interesting scent, and alert their owners to the treed raccoon, staying there until the owners arrive.

For learning a task that doesn't involve raccoons, take my sweet Casey for example.

Our back doors leading to the patio, through the kitchen or the sun room off of my bedroom, have lever handles. The doors open to the inside. However, being outside, Casey learned to open the doors when he wanted to come inside. I'm presuming he learned by watching us use our hands to press down on the lever handle and open the door.

The first time Casey got in the house without anyone letting him in just made me think that the door wasn't closed all the way and he either bumped it or the wind blew it open. I thought that until I saw my coonhound in action. Casey wanted in. He walked over to the back door by the kitchen, stood on his hind legs, and pressed the lever down with his left paw. The door opened and in strolled Casey. Sometimes it took him two, maybe three times tops, to open the door. But he did it every single time he wanted in, providing the door wasn't locked.

Whenever I had to put Casey and Ajax outside, I had to make sure that the doors in the kitchen and sunroom were locked. Otherwise, Casey simply ran over to the other door, opened it, and came back inside. This happened several times, usually when I was running late for work.

Keep in mind that no one ever took the time to show Casey how to open doors. He had to watch. Or else the first time he opened it was by accident and he never forgot that. Either way, Casey was smart.

While Bowie hasn't mastered opening the doors, he knows that when I fill up my tumbler with ice and water I am about to leave. He starts barking, chopping (discussed in Chapter 11), as he knows I'm leaving. Bowie also knows that when I leave, he and Ajax get a dental stick or some other sup-posedly long-lasting treat. Whether they stay in the house or have to suffer through the outdoor elements of 75-degree weather, they happily accept their treat and leaving doesn't present a problem. Bowie doesn't do this at night; only during the day when I put on my shoes and fill up the tumbler.

Even though dogs may learn a behavior or task by observing you, or even another dog, don't expect your coonhound to load the dirty clothes in the washing machine, add soap, and turn it on. Likewise they are not very handy in getting clothes out of the dryer and folding them, although Ajax and Bowie are happy to provide their company to me while I am doing laundry.

Canine intelligence is one reason I don't think you should train your coonhound constantly with treats. This could lead to him thinking that he will sit whenever he wants to, thereby deserving a treat. This sort of "con-ditioning" can also lead to coonhound manipulation, which is a tough hole from which to climb out.

Ajax and Bowie know that they get a treat when they go outside to do their business. Ajax thinks playing with a toy to manipulate me into another treat is a coy, little maneuver. He will play for a few minutes and then trot over to the treat jar and woof at me. Bowie simply loves to play. When he is finished, he will lie down.

However, the evening potty breaks don't always occur at the same time. That would be too easy and only require me getting out of my chair once to let the dogs out and once to let them in. No. Bowie waits. And even though Ajax has already been out, he waits until Bowie dances around and begins dancing, too. Both hounds rush off barking at imagined squirrels (or perhaps there is a scent of squirrel). They won't return to the back door until I'm set-tled back into my chair. So one more treat later and then they get the open hands flashed to them. Sign language for "That's it, boys. No more treats." Both dogs go and lie down in their beds or on the couch.

Intelligence (sometimes aka manipulation) manifests itself into a good memory of knowing where things are. Important things, like the dog treat jar or the leashes. When Casey was ready to go for a walk, he would run over to the wall by the front door where the leashes hang, rattle them, and run back to me. This was repeated until we went on a walk.

You can read more about the intelligence of dogs in Inside of a Dog regarding different intelligent experiments canines were subjected to and the results of their performance and intelligence. It is very interesting. However, as the owner of a Treeing Walker Coonhound, I think each day has the potential to learn about these dogs and their way of thinking.

While dogs can't draw up plans to build a new hospital, I believe that they can problem-solve to a certain degree. One more example of this was with Casey and Ajax.

We used to have feral cats, until the matriarch passed away. I fed them every night on our front porch. If Ajax was in my lap, and Casey wanted to be there, too, he would go to the dining room window and whine or bark. Ajax would hop down and run over to bark at the cats. Sometimes Casey waited for Ajax to get to the window before he hurried back and got in my lap. Other times, he was heading back to me as Ajax was rushing over to get the cats (through the window). Either way, Casey got in my lap and settled in. No one taught him this. He figured it out all on his own. And poor little Ajax fell for it every time, allowing the fever for barking at cats to outweigh staying in my lap.

A Touch of Stubbornness

As we have learned, Treeing Walker Coonhounds are incredibly sweet. They are incredibly smart. And they can be stubborn at times. Don't let this deter you from closing this book and vowing to never own a coonhound. The stubbornness might stem from their intelligence, or their exercise of free will, in not doing what you ask.

They aren't mean about it. Not at all. However, their intelligence and stubbornness create a perfect storm. If this were not enough, be aware that your Treeing Walker Coonhound may experience a sudden, but temporary, onset of deafness along with his stubbornness.

I've never really experienced it with training. Know your limits and your Treeing Walker Coonhound's limits regarding training. If he sits twelve times for you, don't ask him to sit for the thirteenth time. I'd get a little tired of that, too.

My experience with coonhound stubbornness, and subsequent loss of hearing, has been with Casey and Bowie simply having a different idea of how things should go. Namely, when it's time to go outside.

If I had to leave, or it had been several hours since Casey had been outside, and I told him it was time to go out, I was met with complete silence. IF Casey opened his eyes, I was met with a side-eye.

"You talking to me?"

If Casey deigned to raise his head, most of the time he lowered it back down and resumed his nap, ignoring the absurd request his mother just gave him. Most of the time, my presence and proclamation weren't even met with the twitch of a muscle or cock of an ear to indicate that he was remotely interested in what I had to say.

Suffice it to say, that many times I had to gently tug on Casey's collar to get him to go outside. Since he was still in the dog bed, it slid along with us, providing a nice, soft sled for him. When he did decide to stand up, he would sometimes sit back down. If he did actually pay attention to me and walk towards the door, Casey walked like he was trudging through deep water.

Once I was successful in getting my reluctant (i.e. stubborn) coonhound outside, I would discover if he really needed to go outside. Casey would either bound away to pee and bark, or zip over to the other door and let himself back in if the door was unlocked.

Bowie exhibits the same stubbornness and takes his to the full-on bribery level.

"I'll go out if you pay me."

If it is too early in the morning, and Bowie hasn't had his full twelve hours of sleep on the couch, the deafness sets in. Other times, all it takes is the rattle of the treat jar or bag to trump coonhound stubbornness. Bowie is off the couch. I follow through, but when bribery is enforced, the size of the treat is reduced remarkably. Failure to follow through with a treat, even a small one, will notify your Treeing Walker Coonhound that he is being played. This will confound any future attempts to get him outside if he's not ready. Pay to play.

Coonhound Drama

Every dog seems to have their little idiosyncrasies and quirks. The coonhound is no different, just add a big dollop of drama. I don't know if I've ever met a breed of dog that is more dramatic than the Treeing Walker Coonhound. Some of it is sheer enjoyment, but nearly every activity involving a coonhound involves some drama.

Maybe it's because these dogs hunt exuberantly in packs, barking and chopping and baying after their prey, alerting their owners to their whereabouts as well as the whereabouts of whatever critter they treed. That is their job. I imagine a nighttime raccoon hunt is pretty exciting and dramatic. However, coonhounds have managed to bring the drama off the job site and into their every-day existence.

As I just told you, when Casey did manage to drag himself outside at my insistence, sometimes he would have been eligible for an Academy Award for Best Dramatic Actor, taking his time (and mine) to stagger outside.

Playtime with Bowie is a great time for drama, especially in the summer when cicadas and katydids are out. I've watched Bowie jump straight up when he encounters one, or straight back when I pick one up and show it to him.

Sighs of exasperation or "exhaustion" occur on a daily basis, usually when your coonhound hasn't really exerted himself, but must let you know that there's the perception that he has. Take, for example, simply lying down. Many times it will be achieved with much aplomb, involving the coonhound to collapse as if he's been shot. Add some groans for effect. During naps, Bowie will let out a large, deep moan that lasts for several seconds. It always makes me giggle.

Drama can be exhibited in the simple act of sleeping, but not necessarily in a "normal" dog sleeping position. Coonhounds perfected sleeping all tucked up into a perfect circle, the "coonie curl." Your Treeing Walker Coonhound might exhibit a sleeping pattern that might seem like he is posing for a centerfold photo. He might have his back feet tucked up alongside his jowls, curl his head around under a back leg and partially flipped on his side, or any number of other astounding and seemingly unnatural positions for a dog. Or he might stretch out on the whole couch, effectively causing whoever else might be on the couch to relocate. Of course, stretching out on the entire couch also means exaggerating, and emphasizing, a rollover so if you are still sitting on the couch, the Treeing Walker Coonhound torso is now available for belly rubs, pats, and scratches. Casey would always use his forelegs and front paws to pull a human arm down on him if for some reason, the petting ceased.

The drama doesn't end there, though. It really shows itself at mealtime because there is never any way that you can ever get your Treeing Walker Coonhound's supper fixed fast enough.

Usually the drama will ensue when the coonhound clock (keep reading) goes off to alert said hound that it is time to eat. Basically, your coonhound

*Photo Courtesy of
Wendi Sopkin*

will act as if he hasn't eaten in days, even if you feed him twice per day. He's just simply starving. And evidently, you don't seem to care as you are taking your time preparing his meal. Hence, you must be alerted to the state of your coonhound by constant barking (chopping), repeated thrusts of his nose into your thigh (shark bumping), wildly pacing, spinning in circles, and maybe the occasional inspection accomplished by standing on his hind legs to supervise that you are indeed filling his bowl and not fiddling with your phone.

This. Happens. Every. Day.

Drama is effective when there is something unseen by human eyes outside at night. Maybe there's something there and maybe there isn't. Maybe the wind blew something over or is blowing the leaves. Maybe your sibling has been in mom's lap long enough and it's the coonhound's turn. Regardless, it never hurts to alert the whole household, just in case.

When you get your Treeing Walker Coonhound, you might have to call him "Oscar."

Goofballs

Even though drama is strong with coonhounds, Treeing Walker Coonhounds are really big old goofballs. You just never really know what they will do.

Your coonhound might be casually walking through the house, then spy a toy and leap and pounce on it. Bowie does this frequently. Or if he wants a certain toy, he will rummage through his toy box and jump straight up in the air, as if there is a snake in there. I don't know what he sees, but it startles him. But he will get whatever toy he is after and bring it to me to play.

Other times, Bowie will lie in his bed and sniff around. All of a sudden he will jerk his head back in surprise or jump up quickly. Again, I don't know why. Perhaps he got a whiff of how badly his bed smells. Or something is there that he didn't expect.

Bowie has made it a point to get attention by standing next to my son, Justin, then leaping into the air and spinning in a circle. Naturally this elicits laughter as well as the much sought-after petting. If that doesn't work, he will almost turn his head sideways, look up at whoever he is standing next to, and paw them, usually with his left paw. Because it's always all about the coonhound.

Couch Potatoes

Although Treeing Walker Coonhounds are technically athletic, energetic hunting dogs, they adapt well (very well) to a supine position on the couch. If you allow dogs on the furniture, your coonhound will capitalize on this luxury.

When we moved to our house, we got a new couch. It was fake suede and I knew it would be harder to keep clean than our old leather couch. The rule in our house became "No Dogs On The Couch. Ever."

After I rescued Casey, in June of 2017, my husband, David, had back surgery. When the 4th of July rolled around, I went to watch fireworks at a nearby amusement park. When I got home, Casey was sprawled out on the couch, snoring like a buzz saw.

I asked David what was going on. He replied that Casey heard fireworks and it scared him. When he got on the couch, he wasn't afraid. So that was that. My fake suede, dog-hair-free couch was now officially baptized as open for business for my hounds.

Casey was never one to totally monopolize the couch, unless Ajax was there. Casey would happily share with anyone or invite himself up on the couch with you. He would kind of bunny-kick Ajax until poor Ajax jumped down and had to suffer in the Serta dog bed.

Bowie has not had an ounce of trouble acclimating to the couch, either. He's also progressed to my zero-gravity recliner, sharing it with me or completely taking it over when I get up to go to the bathroom. He will happily sleep there or on the couch all night. A coonhound needs his ten hours of beauty sleep after all.

Since Casey and Bowie were both rescues, and Casey was a street dog, someone asked me how long it took them to adjust to coming in the house and also sleeping on the couch.

"About 30 seconds."

In Your Business

Unless your coonhound is outside, you will always have company in the kitchen while you are preparing meals, too. Treeing Walker Coonhounds know what they are doing and they will turn on the charm while you are cooking. They'll also turn on the cuteness with perked-up ears and a wagging tail as well as lay a guilt trip on you with their big, brown, soulful eyes.

Whatever you are doing is important to your Treeing Walker Coonhound. At least for a little while, but more than likely, whatever you are doing will have to be inspected frequently by your coonhound. There could be food involved, a racoon might be close by while you are in the bathroom, you might need help putting on your shoes or typing a book about Treeing Walker Coonhounds on your computer. Your Treeing Walker Coonhound will be an equal opportunity employer and make it his mission to assist you with any of your duties.

If food is involved, your Treeing Walker Coonhound will have a laser focus on your fork and plate, watching every move you make. If you wish to curtail the begging (which is discussed later) or eat in peace, it might be a good time for your coonhound to enjoy the great outdoors, via the backyard, for a while.

Personal Space

When you become the proud parent of a Treeing Walker Coonhound, unless you lock yourself in a room alone, you can basically forget about your very own personal space. It pretty much ceases to exist. Unless your coonhound is deep in sleep somewhere other than your lap, he will probably be wherever you are, whether you are pulling weeds out of the flower bed or going to the restroom. If you think a nice leisurely nap outside on the lounger sounds good, be prepared to scoot over because you're going to have a 60-pound guest.

You will have to decide if your Treeing Walker Coonhound is allowed in your bed or not. David is adamant about not letting dogs in our bed. No exceptions. No room for discussion. The rest of the furniture, except for David's chair, are fair game.

Remember that there is always room for a Treeing Walker Coonhound. Perhaps you are lying on the couch. Alone. If there is a sliver of room between you and the back of the couch, then there is room for your coonhound. It is actually quite cozy as your coonhound will more than likely rest his head on your chest. This was a favorite thing of mine that my sweet Casey did.

If you have to adjust your position, your hound may or may not adjust his position. If you scoot towards the edge of the couch an inch or two, your Treeing Walker Coonhound just gained two inches of real estate. Sitting on the couch with your legs extended the length of the couch has ample opportunities for the coonhound to squeeze between you and the back of the couch, between your legs, or on top of your legs. There are some occasions where your hound needs to curl up so you will need to bend your knees to provide a, preferably, whole seat cushion at the end of your couch for your hound's comfort.

Treeing Walker Coonhounds do not realize that they are not very good windows, especially when you are trying to enjoy a movie. A coonhound silhouette is all that you need to see between you and the television. This happens to me every single night. Bowie hops up in the chair with me, placing his front paws squarely on my left thigh. He has to stand guard for a few minutes to make sure that nothing gets me and to alert me to his presence. I have a grand view of his glorious head and back rather than whatever show I'm watching. After a few minutes he will plop down on my legs with his head on my thigh or the arm of the chair. Or he will fidget until I put my left hand under his head and my right hand is hired to continually pet him while he sleeps. All is suddenly right with the world.

The Coonhound Clock

Your Treeing Walker Coonhound will have his very own personal alarm clock that goes off at appropriate times. Or maybe inappropriate times. Alarm bells at mealtimes are a given, but your coonhound may decide that other times are suitable for other activities. Since mealtime is imperative for your Treeing Walker Coonhound, we will start there.

Bowie gets his medicines in the morning, either in a Pill Pocket or buttered toast. My husband started the buttered toast routine. Bowie likes to sleep in some mornings (after all, he has had an excruciating 10 hours of sleep on the couch), but when he wakes up, if David isn't awake, Bowie will pace and whine around in our room (claws clicking on a hardwood floor make a nice sound while you are trying to sleep) until David gets up. Sometimes, Bowie has to go to David's side of the bed and nose him to make sure that he is getting the message. Since this is their little bonding opportunity, I stay out of the way. If I'm awake and up first, I'll sit in the living room with Bowie. But when he's ready for his toast, he gallops into the bedroom and wakes up David. I'm sorry, but it is really cute and nearly impossible to get mad at him for doing this. Some mornings, Bowie waits on the couch with me for David to bring him his buttered toast.

Supper is around 5:00 p.m., give or take an hour. Or half an hour. Or 10 minutes. Around 4:30, Bowie starts working the crowd. Restlessness sets in and he may start pacing and whining. Now I know that he is not about to die of starvation, so I try and put him off for at least 30 more minutes. Sometimes it works, sometimes it doesn't. What I absolutely cannot do is ask him "Is it time to eat?" Bowie knows this phrase and he begins barking at me, pawing at me, and then runs to the backdoor. The dinner dance has begun. It doesn't end until a bowl of kibble is placed on the patio because I need coonhound supervision and vocal encouragement while I'm scooping up the food, too. If I make the mistake of asking Bowie if it is time to eat before 5:00, I own it and it is time to feed the hounds. Period.

If you live in an area where the time doesn't change in the fall or spring, you are fortunate. The Treeing Walker Coonhound Time-Telling System does not recognize "falling back" or "springing forward." Supper time is supper time. Springing forward isn't as bad as falling back. So when we have to fall back, your coonhound's suppertime, say 6:00, is still his suppertime. Except now it is 5:00. You may need to occupy his time or stay away from the house for about 30 minutes to start getting your coonhound acclimated to the time change.

The same clock will alert the coonhound when it is time to go for a walk. When I had Casey, depending upon the weather, I tried to take him and Ajax for a walk around 3:00 p.m. So just before 3:00, Casey would start barking at me. He would run over to the front door where the leashes are, and rattle the leashes with his nose. If that didn't get my attention, he would run back to me and shark bump me. During the summertime, Casey had no desire to walk outside in the blazing heat, so he learned that our walks would be after his supper when the streets cooled off.

Perhaps you will have other activities that your Treeing Walker Coonhound will become accustomed to doing at a certain time. Never fear. The clock will alert your coonhound, and you, when it is time for the activity. So if you go to the dog park regularly, have scheduled play time or training time, you might think about staggering them at different times, even though it is hard to resist your Treeing Walker Coonhound when he brings you his gingerbread man or headless raccoon to play tug-of-war.

Behavioral Issues

One item that may be in the suitcase from your Treeing Walker Coonhound's former life, or even if there hasn't been a former life he is recovering from, is a fear of thunderstorms. This is an issue that may not be apparent to the rescue agency. Perhaps there were never any storms while the rescue or foster family had the coonhound.

Fear of thunder is an irrational fear. That means there may not be an explanation, or a cure, for it. Your dog is just afraid of the thunder. Or loud noises, like fireworks or gunshots. Many of the Treeing Walker Coonhounds that are dumped out, brought to a rescue, or left at an animal shelter are afraid of gunshots. Hunters don't want a coonhound that is afraid of a gun-shot, so they get rid of the dog, whether it is humanely surrendering him to a shelter or rescue, or cruelly dumping him out in the middle of the country.

The coonhound didn't do anything wrong. He just has a fear of loud noises and shouldn't be punished for that.

Many years ago I had a collie named Rusty. She was absolutely petrified of thunder. As long as she was in the garage or house, she was fine. But if she was out in the yard and heard a distant rumble imperceptible to human ears, she was scratching at the back door. All I had to do was let her inside. That was that.

Photo Courtesy of Jennifer Winkler

Later, little Lucy, our rescue beagle, let us know how absolutely terrified she was of thunder. We tried everything from lavender oil to the doggy Thunder Shirts, to hard drugs with a high street value. Finally, when we moved to our new house, the master bathroom and closet, situated in the middle of the house without windows, became Lucy's safe haven. The first time we had a thunder storm, she simply went back to our bathroom and laid on the rug. I shut the door and the problem was solved! I also moved a little dog bed into our closet just for extra security.

That little dog bed in our closet was also Casey's safe space during storms, too. He was scared of thunder, but not to the point that Lucy was. Still, he was scared enough. Casey would ride out the storm on the couch next to me and when I went to bed, he would either lay in one of the dog beds next to me or go into the closet and curl up in the tiny dog bed. We left it there after Lucy passed away for this very reason.

Luckily Bowie isn't afraid of storms. Ajax is oblivious. I'm grateful for that. It is so hard and scary for the dogs. There is no way to reason with them; just be patient with them and reassure them.

So there may be some baggage that is open to the public, or doesn't reveal itself until weeks or months later. Maybe whatever is in the suitcase just simply stays in the suitcase, tucked away under mounds of love and affection that you are raining down on your Treeing Walker Coonhound, never to be revealed or thought of again.

If your dog has some issues, there's a great chance that they can be resolved with love and patience. You might need a dog trainer, as well. (We called in a professional dog trainer for Casey as discussed in Chapter 7.) The more patience you have with your Treeing Walker Coonhound, the better. Helping your coonhound overcome something may be as simple as speaking kindly to him, or snuggling with him on the couch, instilling and solidifying that bond and reassurance that your dog is truly safe. Your Treeing Walker Coonhound will trust you and become extremely loyal to you. Give him time. And love. And treats. Treats never hurt.

Counter-Surfing

I introduced you to counter-surfing and begging, as well as some remedies for them, in Chapter 7. Counter-surfing is very real, and I think it is particularly inviting and enticing for scent hounds. If some dogs, say a short little dachshund, can't see what is on the counter, he may not even be interested. Oh, he will know that this is where the humans cook and maybe, yummy morsels will be dropped or spilled for his waiting pleasure. But for the most part, if a human isn't present, things on the counter are out of sight, out of mind.

This is not the case with Treeing Walker Coonhounds. They can smell what is there and if they stand on their hind legs, they can see it. Perhaps they can grab it.

I caught Casey in the act of counter-surfing a couple of times. He also felt compelled to do a bit of counter-surfing, and supervising, while I fixed his supper, too. I would tell him "Off!" and he would get back on all fours.

Bowie was a little stealthier. He never really counter-surfs anymore, but the couple of times that he did it were doozies; performed while I was conveniently in another room so he wasn't exactly "caught in the act."

The first time was a few weeks after I got him and just before Thanksgiving. My friend runs a cooking/baking business out of her house. I had ordered a lemon meringue pie, some jelly, and four dozen homemade dinner rolls. I brought them home and put them on the island, then went to my bedroom for something. My son, Justin, was at the dining room table working on homework. Bowie was in his dog bed.

When I came out, Bowie was still in his dog bed, but so was something else. He was chewing on some whitish-yellowish-looking thing. I asked Justin if he gave Bowie anything. He had not.

I walked into the kitchen and a pan of rolls was precariously teetering on the edge of the island. Six of the rolls were gone! I whirled around and discovered what Bowie was intently eating. A half dozen rolls!

"Bowie!" I yelled. But what could I do? He got to enjoy his rolls. I couldn't punish him as I hadn't witnessed the crime. Ajax couldn't reach them. The rolls didn't fall out of the sky. Bowie was guilty, but acquitted due to lack of evidence, resulting in a mistrial.

The other instance involved my search for my chicken nuggets that were on the island in a little cardboard box. They were to be my lunch. However, after I returned from the bathroom, I couldn't find them. I did find a half-eaten cardboard box that once housed eight chicken nuggets, which were in the belly of a very satisfied Treeing Walker Coonhound.

I thought I had scooted the box of nuggets back far enough on the island. Apparently I had not. Not for a Treeing Walker Coonhound anyway.

There are other instances I know of, from other people's experiences, that resulted in the loss of their cornbread, ham, roast, and cake. It sounds funny until it happens to you and your chicken nuggets. Burp.

Begging... and Maybe Some Drool

Treeing Walker Coonhounds are not your typical beggars. They can take begging to new levels. For the most part, Treeing Walker Coonhounds are stealth beggars. Staring intently, with ears perked up to exhibit extreme cuteness (and pity), is their standard modus operandi. Some dogs, other than a Treeing Walker Coonhound, beg by whining. They are such amateurs.

Depending upon how much ice or steel courses through one's veins (there's very little in mine regarding my hounds), the cuteness may work and it may not. Or it may just work once per sitting. Regardless, the charm is turned on. If all else fails, and for a little extra flair, a single loud bark can be emitted. The solo bark results in either a little edible reward or a command to be quiet. But you won't know until you ask. Casey would bark at me, just once, when he thought I didn't know that he was there waiting for a bite of whatever it was that I was eating. Same with Bowie. Just one bark. Just one bite.

There is another form of begging that could be a tad intrusive. I've often said that Treeing Walker Coonhounds are the perfect height for a dog. They aren't too tall and they aren't too short. You don't have to reach down too far to pet your coonhound and when you are walking, your Treeing Walker Coonhound can easily touch your hand with his nose. The average dining room table is perfect to accommodate a certain someone's interested and working-on-overtime nose.

So while you are sitting at your table enjoying your meal, do not be terribly surprised if you discover a Treeing Walker Coonhound's head on your thigh. The coonhound may be sitting or he may be standing. Either way, he is the right height to gaze up at you and watch every move you make, especially when that move involves eating utensils filled with things that can be eaten. If the big soft head on your thigh is too subtle, a shark bump from a coonhound snout on a human elbow connected to a hand holding a forkful of roast more than likely allows said roast to land on the floor or in the mouth of the Treeing Walker Coonhound.

Occasionally, if the human still doesn't grasp the fact that the coonhound is present, a paw might be placed on the thigh to engage eye contact with the human.

Drooling is another specialty of your Treeing Walker Coonhound. To put it simply, some drool a lot and some don't. Most of the drool I encountered with Casey and Bowie involved wet drops of drool on the floor next to me. Occasionally it ends up on my thigh. No puddles, just drops.

However, there are coonhounds who have, perhaps, some excessive drool ("shoe laces)" hanging down, dangling and swinging, from both sides of their jowls. Complement that with some head shaking and the shoe laces wrap around their head, looking like your coonhound has been splattered with meringue or smeared with a little bit of cake icing.

Treeing Walker Coonhounds do not generally produce drool just for existing, as some breeds do, but rather from an experience, such as intensely desiring a piece of food or barking and barking at something in the yard. Drool is harmless. It wipes up easily with a paper towel. I like to believe that it has healing powers like a mother's spit does.

Judgement Day

In the next chapter, you will learn about the eyes and vision of your Treeing Walker Coonhound. However, there is another fact that you probably won't find in any books or articles about canine vision.

Coonhounds judge.

Yep. You read that right. They will judge you.

It doesn't matter if he is sitting, standing, or lying down. Judgment happens. You will be judged by your Treeing Walker Coonhound on more than one occasion.

I like to think that they don't mean to judge, but I think that they actually do.

Judging involves the coonhound eye. It can be an incredulous look implying that he can't believe you aren't giving him another treat. Judgement can also be in the form of a side-eye, whereas the coonhound is acknowledging your presence but not even attempting to process your command. At the current moment, you have been deemed to not be listened to, but you have been noticed. Another form of coonhound judgement is the half-closed eye stare. This might occur if you dare not give your hound a bite, or all, of what you are eating, or if you ask him to get off the couch, go outside, or basically anything else that he doesn't want to do. Oh if you are eating something, at first you will get the warm, large, soulful, pitiful, brown-eyed treatment. Failure on your part to provide sustenance to the coonhound will impart the judging eyes.

Get ready. You have been warned.

CHAPTER 10
Those Ears and Eyes

The Treeing Walker Coonhound Ear

You know that your coonhound can smell better than you can. He can also hear better than you can, too. About four times better.

Your Treeing Walker Coonhound, like all dogs, is born deaf and will develop his hearing over the next few weeks. However, when he is at his prime peak of age and health, your Treeing Walker Coonhound might be able to hear sounds up to 60,000 Hertz ("ultrasonic" sounds, such as a dog whistle that makes an inaudible sound to us but is crystal clear to your coonhound). Hence your coonhound can hear small rodents squeaking in a wood pile or under the ground. Humans can hear sounds up to 20,000 Hertz. This varies with age, and as we get older, our hearing diminishes. It does with dogs, too.

Add to this that your hound has 18 muscles in each ear which allows him to move his ears to better direct, orient, and process the sound. Your coonhound's ears can act and move independently as well

HELPFUL TIP
Watch Out For Ticks!

Ticks can be a nuisance for any dog, but the TWC's long floppy ears make an excellent hiding spot for these troublesome pests. Because ticks carry disease, it's important to remove them as soon as possible to prevent pathogen transmission. The transmission of diseases such as Lyme disease, ehrlichiosis, and babesiosis can happen as soon as three to six hours after your dog has been bitten, and the sooner you remove the tick, the less likely it is that your dog will become sick. To remove a tick, it's best to use fine-pointed tweezers and grasp the tick as close to the skin as possible. Pull the tick slowly and gently straight away from the skin so that the entire tick is removed. You can also purchase a tick-removal hook for this purpose. After the tick has been removed, be sure to wash your hands thoroughly, clean the bite site with rubbing alcohol, and disinfect any tools you used.

Photo Courtesy of
Lisa Morgan

(like their nostrils). When your coonhound tilts his head, perhaps when you make a funny sound, he is perhaps trying to hear better or determine from where the sound is coming or even what is making that sound. He looks pretty cute doing it, too, even if he's not trying to turn on the charm.

The ears, specifically the pinnae (the outer ear, whether it is floppy like a coonhound ear, erect like a collie ear, or bat-shaped like a corgi ear) also act as a form of communication to you and other dogs. Perked up ears (the cuteness factor ears) mean that your coonhound is alert and paying attention. Cocking an ear back means he is listening to something that may not be right by him, but he has heard it and it is getting his attention. Droopy ears can imply fear or dread, noted if you are scolding your hound. Droopy ears can also mean that your dog is not feeling well, is in pain, or could be sad. Relaxed ears, not necessarily intentionally droopy, means that your coonhound is comfortable and at ease, friendly, and even happy.

Dogs with erect and pointy ears, like German Shepherds, may pin their ears back when they are angry and coming after something. It's the "I mean business!" warning and can also indicate fear or even submission. Erect ears, on the alert, help them pay attention to their surroundings. German Shepherds, collies and other breeds with erect ears usually have guarding and protecting jobs to do, so they are bred to hear things and be on the alert. Our droopy-eared hound friends developed their droopiness and floppiness through domestication as they aren't generally dependent upon their hearing for survival like their wild cousins, wolves, foxes and coyotes, are.

Your coonhound's ears allow him to process sounds. This means that he literally has selective hearing. You will learn this by default anyway, but it also means that he might hear the television, normal chatter, birds, and the wind at the same time while he is snoozing on your couch. He will filter and evaluate these sounds and determine if they are important. More than likely none of them are too important for his survival on the sofa. But if you rattle the treat jar, inner coonhound alarms go off and the signal that this is a vital sound to pay attention to is triggered. Your coonhound will wake up from a snoring, dead sleep and be at the treat jar in an instant. Survival.

Even though your coonhound can process sounds, he might have trouble interpreting or distinguishing words that are similar in sound. As was discussed in the training section, be aware of your words. "Heel" and "Here" or "Go" and "No" might sound very similar to your coonhound.

Embrace the Floppiness

Probably one of the first things anyone notices about a Treeing Walker Coonhound (besides their beauty) is their long floppy ears, sometimes referred to as "pendant ears." While floppy ears certainly enhance the cuteness factor of your coonhound, the floppy ears actually have a purpose.

You know that you have a scent hound. That was discussed thoroughly in Chapter 8. However, whether your coonhound is on a hot trail or simply sniffing around his yard, his ears are helping him sort out smells.

When your coonhound has his nose to the ground, sucking air and smells in his nose and pushing them out the sides, his head is down. His ears help stir

Photo Courtesy of Emily Vacek

up scents, directing them to his nose where they can be processed and evaluated. When your hound pushes the air and scents out through the side slits of his nose, the scents travel to his long ears, which are dangling down specifically to catch and trap those scents! Think of sweeping dirt into a dust pan. That is what your coonhound does with his ears when he's sniffing the ground.

Even though you now know that your Treeing Walker Coonhound has a specific purpose for his floppy ears, you will also notice how incredibly soft his ears are. If you need to relax and lower your blood pressure, get your hound in your lap and twirl his velvety soft ears around in your fingers. Stroke them and feel the softness. He won't mind it one bit and you will benefit as well.

The long, soft, floppy ears have one other purpose. It may not necessarily be a scientific fact, but it's there nonetheless. Your coonhound's ears enhance his cuteness factor and make him absolutely adorable.

Big Brown Marbles

No doubt you have gazed lovingly into your Treeing Walker Coonhound's big, round, brown eyes. And he will gaze back, looking intently and lovingly, into your eyes. He recognizes you visually as well as by smell and sound!

Most dogs have brown eyes. There are a few exceptions of course, with some dogs such as Australian Shepherds, having blue eyes, one blue eye, or light blue flecks in their brown or blue eyes. Dogs tend to not have much white (sclera) around their eyes, either. For the most part, hounds have brown eyes.

The pupils, the black spots in the middle of the eyes of your Treeing Walker Coonhound, do not dilate or contract like a human or feline pupil does. Even if the light changes from dark to bright, the pupils of your hound remain fixed at about three to four millimeters. Contrast that to a human pupil which can expand to nine millimeters or contract to one millimeter.

Human and canine eyes have rods, photoreceptors that distinguish degrees of light. Dogs have more rods than humans do (approximately three times more), which helps them see things in motion as well as in low light. This is very important if you make your canine living as a hunter. Your hound doesn't need to see the various shades of green leaves; he needs to see the critter moving among the leaves. Night vision is important for a Treeing Walker Coonhound since the business of hunting raccoons occurs at night. Your coonhound can see seven times better than you can in low light. You might see a light shining in a window in the distance; your coonhound will see the lamp.

The tapetum lucidum at the back of the retina reflects the ample light that comes through the pupils. The light is bounced back and forth and not absorbed by the rods and cones (another photoreceptor). It allows whatever is out there to be given the chance to be seen. The tapetum lucidum is why your coonhound looks like he has alien eyes in photographs.

Your coonhound's eyes are not located in the center of his head like a human's, but more to the sides. Not as much as a horse, who can see nearly 360 degrees, which is necessary if you are a prey animal. But your coonhound, who is basically nearsighted, can see about 250 degrees around him.

Dog vision is about 20/75, compared to the "normal" 20/20 vision of humans. This means that your coonhound can see at 20 feet what a human sees at 75 feet. He will have trouble seeing something clearly in front of him, such as his toy. It simply isn't as in focus for him as it is for us. His vision, looking straight down at something, will be rather grainy and not as sharp or in focus as it would be for us. However, if you are 75 feet away from your hound and wave your arms or start running, he will see you.

Your Treeing Walker Coonhound can see more movement to the sides than you can. If you throw his toy straight ahead of him, he won't see it as well as he will if you throw it to the side. Your coonhound can see motion at a distance up to twenty times better than you can. Consider this factor if you

Photo Courtesy of
Tina Fowble

are teaching your Treeing Walker Coonhound hand signals. Make a wide, sweeping or extending motion that he can see much better than a small hand signal right in front of him.

The ability to see motion at a distance, and in low light, are perfect for your raccoon-hunting hound.

Your Treeing Walker Coonhound Isn't Colorblind

Contrary to popular belief, your Treeing Walker Coonhound is not colorblind nor does he just see in shades of gray. While your hound won't be able to see all of the colors in the rainbow, he can see blue/violet and greenish-yellow as well as distinguishing different shades of gray.

The mnemonic device used to remember the rainbow color spectrum, ROYGBIV, doesn't apply to your coonhound's vision. Instead of seven beautiful colors (even though indigo has basically been removed), he sees an almost brownish-green, brownish-gold, yellow, yellowish-gold, cobalt blue, and dark cobalt blue. Not exactly the stuff that comprises a beautiful photo. But it works for the dog. Think of it as sepia vision.

Cones are the photoreceptors in the eye that are responsible for seeing color. Human eyes have three cones, responding to the red, blue and green wavelengths. Dogs have two cones for blue and green/yellow. Your coonhound won't see pink or red as they aren't vibrant colors for your coonhound. But reds and pinks will appear as various shades of green, yellow, or even a shade of brown, based on their brightness due to the amount of light reflected towards them. So buying your Treeing Walker Coonhound a red ball or hot pink fuzzy animal toy is strictly for your viewing pleasure.

Throw in Some Floppy Skin

Even though your cute little Treeing Walker Coonhound puppy will have loose and wrinkly skin, when he is around five years of age he will start developing a thick neck roll. It is very pliable and loose and doesn't mean that your hound is fat.

This neck roll is important for your coonhound in the event that he gets into a fight with another animal, say a raccoon. It acts as a layer of protection. If some other critter gets ahold of the neck roll, then they are less likely to get to the vulnerable neck which contains the jugular veins and carotid arteries.

In addition to protecting your coonhound, his neck roll as well as wrinkles on his face, help trap scents. He can pack these scents around with him as he goes so he has a reminder about what trail he is on and who or what he is tracking. And you thought the wrinkles were just to enhance the cuteness factor!

As an aside, when Bowie sits down, he has a cute little fold of skin right above his rear end. It's a large wrinkle that makes its way down to his bottom and adds to his cuteness factor. My husband said it is a fat roll. It's not! It's just more floppy skin, giving Bowie a little more character and making him cuter.

Jowls

All dogs have jowls, just like we have cheeks. Jowls hang on each side of the head and mouth. The jowls also contain whiskers, which serve as an extra sensory device for your Treeing Walker Coonhound. Some dogs, such as bloodhounds or mastiffs, have more prominent jowls.

Dogs that were bred to fight, such as bulldogs and mastiffs, have larger, droopier jowls to protect them from other dogs or animals grabbing and biting at their face. It is much better to have the jowl grabbed than the eyes or nose. So jowls act as a protective layer for the face. If your coonhound comes into contact with a raccoon, again, it is better if the raccoon bites the jowl than some other more sensitive area. Drool on the jowl also causes it to be slick and hard to hold on to. Additionally, the jowls aren't as sensitive as other areas (not to imply that it doesn't hurt if something bites your coonhound's jowls) and do not have as many blood vessels and nerve endings as other areas. So your coonhound probably won't have a mortal wound from a bite on his jowl.

Jowls also provide an extra space to trap air for dogs swimming in the water. Newfoundlands and Labradors have large jowls for this purpose because they are very good swimmers and enjoy being in the water. When they are retrieving something from the water, they can breathe easier while swimming with the ample air trapped in their jowls.

As for your scent hound, the jowls serve a purpose for him, too, in that they retain scents. In addition to the jowls, some dogs such as Basset hounds, bloodhounds, and your Treeing Walker Coonhound, also have a dewlap. The dewlap is the collections of loose skin folds under the chin. When your coonhound is on the trail of something, his jowls, like his ears, help stir up scents. Scents can become trapped on his jowls and dewlap, again, providing him with a constant source of the scent he is following.

Of course, drool can drip from the jowls, too.

Your Treeing Walker Coonhound gets more fascinating by the minute!

CHAPTER 11
Vocalization

Barking Redefined

Photo Courtesy of
Wendi Sopkin

Whatever dog you get is going to bark (unless it is a Basenji). Your Treeing Walker Coonhound will bark. I'm not going to kid you. It's the honest truth. But don't despair. He won't bark constantly and fortunately, he can be trained to keep his yap shut if you aren't hunting raccoons.

Barking is one way a dog communicates. Body language, ear expression, and urinating (for leaving scents and information for other dogs) are other ways of canine communication. Barking is verbal communication between your coonhound and you or other dogs.

The uniqueness of Treeing Walker Coonhounds extends into their world of self-expression. They don't just bark. They have several forms of barking, taking barking to a whole new, and fascinating, level.

Chopping

I might as well be upfront about it. Treeing Walker Coonhounds have a chopping bark. Chopping is used to get your attention, like as to the whereabouts of your coonhound who has just treed a raccoon for you, or if you are a little slow about getting his supper fixed. It is useful when your coonhound wants something right now and can be considered as argumentative. But for the most part, your Treeing Walker Coonhound is telling you something or giving you information that you just aren't quite grasping. So you have to be reminded.

> **FUN FACT**
> **Origins**
>
> Treeing Walker Coonhounds are descended from English Foxhounds and were referred to as English Foxhounds until 1945, when breeders deviated from this standard. Modern Treeing Walker Coonhounds still maintain similar coloring to the Walker Foxhound, one of the breeds from which TWCs are descended, and are known for their clear, ringing bugle.

Repeatedly. Quickly. In succession. Think rapid fire talking. "Hey!Hey!Hey!Hey! Times 10.

Chopping seems to be unique in coonhounds. While watching the Treeing Walker Coonhound in the Westminster Dog Show, the announcer made it a point to mention the chopping. Chopping has made the Big Time!

Baying

A coonhound bay is not a howl. It's not quite a bark, either. It's more like a combo. It can be almost mournful-sounding. Personally, I think it is hauntingly beautiful.

Baying is useful when on the hunt for raccoons, running through the woods to alert the human that the coonhound is doing his job and also to inform said human of the coonhound's whereabouts. Baying is best performed while standing, to announce what is going on, or standing on the hind legs with the front legs on the tree that is occupied by the raccoon. The Treeing Walker Coonhound will probably throw his head back in an almost unnatural position for good measure.

While supper is being carried to the waiting Treeing Walker Coonhound (the chopping has served its purpose in that the meal has been prepared), it never hurts to bay a little to let the human know that the food is very much appreciated.

Defense Bark

Your Treeing Walker Coonhound will consider it his job to protect his home and announce the presence of an intruder, whether it is the plumber, the landscapers next door at the neighbor's house, or the elementary kid selling wrapping paper.

The defense bark is a very deep and loud "What are you doing here?" bark. It is useful at the front door until proper introductions have been made or running up and down the fence barking at a deer or yard guy. Sometimes a bit of chopping can be thrown in for good measure.

Barking at Whatever

Our yard has a designated Bark Zone where Bowie has worn a trail barking at things unseen, but definitely things that left a scent. We have a bird feeder in the Bark Zone as well and I discovered that Bowie really doesn't care for crows and will chase them. Perhaps he is smelling the crows or squirrels or mice. Who knows? But he will bark and bark and bark with his nose to the ground, making his figure eight pattern on the trail he has worn.

This is fine for a little while. Let him have some fun and be a coonhound. However, when we are gone and Bowie and Ajax are in the yard, I don't want him barking his head off constantly.

As I mentioned, we have bark collars. Bowie seems to have developed an immunity, or a fondness, to the beep and vibration. We had to step it up a level.

David ordered an ultrasonic beeper. He installed it on the tree by the bird feeder and when Bowie barks, it emits a sound that humans can't hear. There is also a remote for use in the house when Bowie decides he doesn't have anything better to do so he barks.

One press of the button and Bowie was on the couch pressed up against me. He wouldn't have anything to do with David for a while. David apologized but Bowie stopped barking. We have only had to turn on the ultrasonic beeper once outside. That was enough and Bowie got in the dog house. So we turned it off.

I still let him have his coonhound fun in the Bark Zone. But when we tell him enough is enough and to "HUSH!" making a sweeping motion with a fist, Bowie picks up on that and stops barking.

Don't think that Treeing Walker Coonhounds bark constantly. They don't. They just have to inform everyone of what they are smelling or what ran through the yard. They are informative like that.

Photo Courtesy of
Keith Bentley

Photo Courtesy of Jennifer Blankenship

Backtalk

On occasion, you might tell your Treeing Walker Coonhound something that he really doesn't want to hear. If you need him to be quiet, back up, or heaven forbid, *wait* for something like his supper, you might be met with a little bit of backtalk. It probably won't be chopping, but he will bark at you. Add to that perhaps a little whiny "Rrrrr." Translated it means, "Oh, come on," or "For Pete's sake. Really?" It isn't a growl, but he will let you know he isn't too pleased with what is going on right now, that he is present and aware of the situation, and you need to get your act together pronto. If you say something to him, he will reply back. Once he gets his way, all is right with the world.

Another form of coonhound backtalk is really sweet. I have been the wonderful recipient from Casey and Bowie. It's pleasant and quiet. Most of the time it happens when Bowie is in my lap or standing in my lap. I will talk to him and tell him how pretty he is and how much I love him. He replies with a little strained exhale, adding a soft whistle for an extra touch to get me right in the feels. It almost has a quiet wheeze about it. The best way I can describe it (and I know that you are going to try this) is to close your mouth and make the very first basic movement and sound of clearing your throat. Of course the best way is to simply get your coonhound in your lap and talk to him. Then you will hear it. It's not loud and sometimes barely perceptible to our ears. But your hound is talking back to you in a good way. He's letting you know that he hears you and he likes what he is hearing. And probably that he loves you, too.

Singing

Some people may prefer the term "howling." Howling, in my opinion, is when there is a siren in the distance. I prefer "singing" because Casey always sang a song to me when I left for work and when I got home.

Casey was easy to get to sing, too. I could sit on the couch with him, or my sons could. One of us would start emitting a low, throaty howling noise. Casey absolutely could not resist. He would throw his head back and let loose with his song.

Although Bowie has never sang me a song, there's no reason why your Treeing Walker Coonhound won't sing to you. Enjoy it. Sing along. Make a video of it because you will never ever regret it.

Photo Courtesy of
Jessica Alpert

Calling

Your Treeing Walker Coonhound may call to you if he knows you are in the front yard and he's in the back yard. It is pretty much a single, loud bark. It will be repeated, but not with the frenzy of chopping. Think of it as locator device or the coonhound is calling you from his cell phone.

Casey called to me right after I rescued him. Casey and Lucy were on leashes and Ajax was running free in the magical place called the front yard. Normally, Ajax won't run away. However on this particular day, it was the middle of July and I had just finished teaching a yoga class. I was wearing yoga clothes and slip-on sandals. My son Ian was with me. I didn't have my phone with me nor did I have a bottle of water. Ajax decided to chase the deer that were in our neighbor's yard. Off they went! Ian took Casey and Lucy in the house and I took off, to the woods, in my little non-woods shoes, screaming like a banshee for Ajax to come back.

Casey kept me grounded and oriented with his consistent calling to me with his deep barks. He was letting me know where he was and may have been telling his goofy brother to get home. His calling was what helped me navigate back through the brush to get back home so I could get in the car and go look for Ajax. It also helped me as I had to quickly shower to get the chiggers off and then change into jeans and boots, grab my phone and water, and head back out to look for Ajax. Casey kept the calling going until Justin called and said Ajax came home. I know Ajax heard Casey. But my sweet Treeing Walker Coonhound kept calling to me until I opened the gate and stepped into the back yard. What a good boy!

I also want to share with you another calling, a very different calling, that Casey used for me. The night before I had to say goodbye to my sweet Casey, when he couldn't get up and I knew he was not going to survive his cancer. I showered and crawled in bed. Casey was in the living room and started calling to me, with loud, mournful barks that were more like yips. I got up and came into the living room. He kept calling to me until I was able to get down on the floor with him (I was about six weeks out from a hip replacement). Casey stopped. Casey's calling reminded me of puppies when they don't have their eyes opened and are calling for their mama. I know that he was calling for me, the only human mama he had ever known. I stayed with him all night in the living room.

Treeing Walker Coonhounds are noisy, but they are very special dogs. Very special indeed.

CHAPTER 12

Health of Your Treeing Walker Coonhound

Grooming

Bowie and Ajax love going to see Kristen, their groomer. They go nuts when I turn right out of our housing addition because they know where we are going (and donuts are involved, too). I like supporting a small business. I also like the thought of not having to scrub my bathtub after bathing dogs.

I had to do that once, after Bowie decided to play in the mud after a particularly hard rainstorm. I called and called for him and finally, as I was about to panic, he peeped around our outdoor fireplace. I called again and he stepped out. My Treeing Walker Coonhound was no longer tri-color; rather he was all brown. Muddy brown. Muddy brown because brown mud was literally dripping off Bowie. It was fun picking up a 60-pound ball of mud and putting it in my bathtub. Bowie didn't move a muscle while I was bathing him. He loves to be petted so two hands rubbing and massaging him was all right.

Barring any encounters with a skunk or mud puddle, your Treeing Walker Coonhound can get by with a bath every two to three months, depending upon if they stink. Some coonhounds will start to smell after a couple of months, some won't. So if your hound develops an undesirable odor, give him a bath. Get a shampoo that is made for dogs and won't burn his eyes. You will also want to make sure that you dry the insides of his floppy ears thoroughly as wet inner ears covered by floppy outer ears can be a breeding ground for bacteria and yeast.

After his bath, you can spritz your coonhound with a nice doggy spray to make him smell nice. He can also be spritzed intermittently between baths to keep him smelling fresh and less "coonhoundy."

Shedding

Even though your Treeing Walker Coonhound has short, easy-to-manage hair, he will shed. Quite a bit. I've gotten used to teaching my yoga classes with a bit of Treeing Walker Coonhound hair on my pants and shirt. I have a cover for my couch and we also invested in a Roomba, which keeps the dog hair swept up on a daily basis.

Bowie doesn't shed as much as Ajax. Beagles definitely know how to shed and you can wipe off handfuls of hair from them. I have not found that to be the case with Treeing Walker Coonhounds. But I'm not going to lie. They do shed. If you don't mind dog hair here and there, you won't mind having a Treeing Walker Coonhound in the house.

Photo Courtesy of
Alie Roberts

Claws

I don't like trimming dog claws. I'm always afraid I'll cut them off in a quick; even the white nails where I can see the bloodline.

Most Treeing Walker Coonhounds will have white feet and white claws. There may be some brown, tan or black speckles and spots on their legs, so maybe a claw or two will have some pigmentation. Even though your coonhound probably has mostly white claws, you still need to be careful when trimming his claws.

If your Treeing Walker Coonhound sits still, it should be relatively simple for you to trim his claws. You will want to invest in a good dog nail trimmer, not a cheap one. And make sure that it stays sharpened. If it is dull, then you might have to try to snip at the claws several times.

- Have your coonhound sit or even lie down to trim his nails. If he doesn't mind you touching his feet, that will help this process go much smoother.
- Lift a paw and select a claw to trim. Remember that you should only pull your hounds leg forward or push it backwards. Their shoulders and hips aren't built to extend outward.
- Take the claw trimmer and insert the claw into it, going just below the blood line. With white claws, you will be able to see the pink bloodline in the claw. Black claws make this much harder and scarier!
- Squeeze the trimmer and snip off the end of the claw.
- Give your coonhound praise after each snip. Maybe give him a small treat after every few snips, too.
- Don't forget to trim the dew claws, the claws on the sides of his front legs. They can grow and curl into his leg.
- The claws don't have to be short. You might just snip the ends and call it a day. Then when the claws start growing out, you can snip the ends off again.
- You don't want to be in a hurry, but you don't want this to take all day either. Boredom or even fear and anxiety might set in with your coonhound, making the job of trimming his claws harder.
- If your coonhound is behaving, you might even file the rough edges of his claws. That way, when he gets in your lap, his claws won't snag your clothes. Snagging his claws could also rip his claws and hurt him. So ensure that there aren't any rough edges on his claws.

If you want to really play it safe, purchase an electronic grinder and simply file his claws down. It doesn't take long and there is almost a zero

Photo Courtesy of Elena Amjady

chance of you hurting your hound. He will need to sit still, even though this isn't a painful process at all. If you have a groomer, check and see if she has a grinder and will grind down your coonhound's claws.

You may discover that your coonhound's claws grow extremely fast, or maybe they don't. Bowie's grow fast whereas Casey's did not. Taking your hound on walks will help wear down his claws. You don't want to get to the point where the claws start curling under, causing problems with walking as well as growing into the foot pads.

If you are hesitant to trim your Treeing Walker Coonhound's claws yourself, have your veterinarian or groomer do it for you. Every two or three months should be fine, unless you notice the claws are really long.

Skin

Just as in humans, the skin on your Treeing Walker Coonhound is his largest organ and the first line of defense against dirt, infection, sunlight, other unwanted things, and water loss.

Most of your coonhound's body will be covered in hair, which provides warmth and extra protection from the sun and outdoor elements. Dogs have compound hair follicles, meaning that several hairs can come from the same follicle. This helps your coonhound trap the air and stay warm. There are some exposed skin areas, such as the inside of his ears, toe pads, and lower belly.

For the most part, your coonhound should have healthy skin. Keeping your hound hydrated as well as feeding him a food that contains proper proteins, healthy fatty acids (Omega-3 and Omega-6), as well as vitamins A, E, and zinc will ensure that his skin and coat stay shiny and healthy. Your veterinarian can recommend a supplement that contains the Omegas (fish oil) and a vitamin as well. Most supplements and vitamins are flavored so your coonhound will think he's getting one more daily treat.

Although there are many skin conditions found in dogs, I will list a few that could potentially affect your coonhound. If you notice your hound scratching a lot, check where he is scratching and see if it looks red or inflamed, maybe bloody or crusty. If you discover unhealthy-looking skin, take your hound to the veterinarian.

- **ALLERGIES:** Your Treeing Walker Coonhound could develop allergies from grasses, pollen, his dog shampoo, bug bites, his food, fleas and ticks, or other things. It is a very good idea to have your veterinarian check out your Treeing Walker Coonhound. Food allergies might be simple enough to remedy by simply switching the food that you feed your dog, possibly buying a grain-free food. Your hound may need to be on medication or even a daily dose of Benadryl. In some instances, a steroid such as prednisone may be needed. My beagle Rascal had an allergic reaction to Bermuda grass and had to be on prednisone in the summer. When we moved, our house had a different type of grass and the problem was immediately solved!

- **HOT SPOTS:** If you notice bare spots on your hound that appear to be sore and inflamed, he probably has a hot spot. Your veterinarian will prescribe a cream or possibly even a medication or shot for your hound to help him get relief and healing from his hot spots. To date, none of my beagles or coonhounds have had hot spots. My collie did have them; she got them every summer and had to be treated for them.

- **YEAST INFECTIONS:** Although yeast infections may be more common in the ears, and that will be discussed later in this chapter, yeast infections can occur on the skin. Casey had a yeast infection on his right thigh. It itched and he chewed around on it. The white hair on his thigh turned a brownish color from the yeast. Fortunately, the veterinarian prescribed a generic Gentamicin spray that cleared up the yeast infection.

- **MANGE:** The ultimate skin disease for dogs is caused by mites. Mange comes in two varieties: demodectic and sarcoptic. If you suspect that your coonhound has mange, take him to the veterinarian as soon as possible. Your veterinarian will conduct a skin scrape biopsy to determine if it is mange and what type. Treatment will be in the form of medicated baths (dips) or injections. Your coonhound will not be immune from mange after he contacts it. He can get it again if he is in contact with the mites or an infected animal. Any diagnosis of mange will require you to sanitize all dog bedding, toys, furniture, collars, dog houses, food bowls, harnesses, and whatever else your hound has played with, eaten out of, or slept on. Note that the mites can bite humans and cause itching!

  - Demodectic mange, or Demodex, may start out as a bald spot, not necessarily inflamed but it will be itchy. Left untreated, it will spread, possibly even to your hound's feet (demodectic ppododermatitis). Demodectic mange is not life-threatening nor is it contagious; however it will cause your hound to be extremely uncomfortable and itchy. This can affect his overall health, causing anxiety from the constant itching and could lead to weight loss, fever, and swollen lymph nodes.

  - Sarcoptic mange, or scabies, is more severe and contagious from dog to dog. Dogs with sarcoptic mange will be unhealthy and require veterinary care immediately and will need to be quarantined. Sarcoptic mange can be passed from a mother dog to her puppies. The mites that cause sarcoptic mange can survive up to 21 days away from their hosts in temperatures of 50-59°F or up to six days in temperatures of 68-77°F.

Ear Maintenance

Keeping your Treeing Walker Coonhound's ears clean is very important. Dogs have an L-shaped ear canal, which protects the inner ear but also allows the accumulation of wax, dirt, and debris, which can cause infections. Your coonhound's adorable, long, floppy ears are a good way to trap dirt and bacteria and crud inside his ears.

Ear infections are at the top of the list for visiting the veterinarian. Regular cleaning of your coonhound's ears can prevent an infection and a trip to the vet. Never use alcohol in your dog's ears. If the ears are red or swollen, the alcohol will burn and hurt your coonhound. A damp cloth or cotton ball can be used as well as ear wipes made for dogs.

If you notice him scratching his ears a lot, or yelping when you rub his ears, he needs to go to the vet. It could be allergies or an infection. If you notice a brown, smelly discharge in your coonhound's ears, he probably has a yeast infection and needs to see the veterinarian. If your coonhound enjoys swimming, make sure that you dry the inside of his ears after his dip in the pool or river or pond.

Heartworms

Heartworms are a horrible thing to happen to any dog. Any dog is susceptible to this disease. They are transmitted to your coonhound when he is bitten by a mosquito that has already bitten an infected dog (or even a fox, coyote or wolf). The female heart worms produce the microscopic baby worms (microfilaria). When the mosquito bites an infected animal, it ingests the microfilaria and after 10-14 days, they develop into larvae. When the mosquito bites your coonhound, it will deposit saliva that contains the larvae and they will enter your coonhound's bloodstream. It takes about six months for the heartworms to mature into foot-long, spaghetti-looking worms that invade all areas of the heart, lungs and arteries of your hound. Heartworms can only be transmitted by mosquitoes; they aren't contagious from dog to dog.

Photo Courtesy of
Rebecca Cummins

If your coonhound is not on heartworm preventative and becomes infected with heartworms, he will develop a cough, exhibit fatigue, loss of appetite and weight, and will not feel like running and playing.

Heartworm disease can be avoided entirely by having your coonhound checked when he is six to seven months of age. Puppies under the age of six months don't need to be tested and can be started on heartworm preventative.

Your veterinarian will do a simple blood test and look for the presence of microfilaria, adult heartworms, or the antigen from heartworm proteins. Antigen tests can produce a false negative if only male or immature female worms are present, if your dog is less than five months old, there is not a large infestation of heartworms (and the infestation will grow if your hound is thought to be heartworm-free and isn't treated), or if the test itself has some discrepancies (not performed correctly, manufacturer defects). If no microfilaria are detected, your coonhound needs to be started on a preventative in the form of a monthly chewable or a topical liquid rubbed between the shoulders every month. Your Treeing Walker Coonhound should be checked annually for the presence of heartworms, even if he's on preventative.

If you live in an area near water sources or with a large population of mosquitoes, having your yard sprayed, as well as having your coonhound on a heartworm preventative will keep him heartworm-free. Warmer tropical climates will have mosquito populations for a longer period of time so that increases your coonhound's chances of being infected if he isn't on a heartworm preventative.

Should your hound have heartworms, there are two types of treatment available, a fast-kill and a slow-kill method. The fast-kill method, adulticide, takes three months to complete. Due to the presence of heartworms in your hound's heart, or the possibility that your coonhound develops blood clots from the aggressive adulticide treatment, your coonhound will need to remain completely inactive during this time, which means no exercise, playing, or going on walks.

The longer and less-aggressive treatment involves a monthly topical dose of Advantage Multi® (dosage is based on the weight of your coonhound) and doxycycline. Doxycycline is an antibiotic that will be given orally to your hound, usually on a daily basis for one month.

Casey and Bowie both got the Advantage Multi® treatment. Casey was heartworm-free in six months. Bowie had a nasty infestation of heartworms. His veterinarian could see the heartworms on x-rays, in his lungs and heart. The worms were so bad in his lungs that they damaged Bowie's lungs, causing Bowie to have a strong, hacking, strangling cough as well as short-ness of breath. Short walks were almost too much for Bowie. The fast-kill and aggressive treatment was determined to be too aggressive for Bowie. With the slow-kill Advantage Multi® treatment, it took Bowie a year and a half to become heartworm-free. He and Ajax continue to be on Advantage Multi® as a heartworm preventative. And they get their annual heartworm test to make sure that they stay negative.

Whether you opt for an oral or topical heartworm preventative, make sure that you indeed give your Treeing Walker Coonhound his preventative each month. If you miss a month or two, you may need to get him rechecked, especially if it is mosquito season. Additionally, make sure that your coon-hound doesn't spit out his oral medication when you aren't looking. They can become very good at this. If you use the topical prescription, make sure that it gets down to the skin and you don't give your hound a bath for a few days afterward.

Fleas

I don't think I need to elaborate on how disgusting fleas and ticks are, whether you are a human or a Treeing Walker Coonhound. Fleas are tiny insects that can jump on your coonhound, bite him, and suck his blood. They can also jump on you bite you, and suck your blood. Your coonhound could be allergic to flea bites and may develop irritated or scabby areas where the bites occurred. If fleas weren't bad enough, they can also transmit diseases. Think Bubonic Plague, courtesy of the fleas on the rats.

Adult fleas live on your coonhound, enjoying his blood and laying their eggs. A single female flea can lay up to 2,000 eggs! The eggs may hatch any-where from one day to ten days. They are easily spread from dog to dog, dog to human, in your house and in your yard. The eggs hatch and become larvae, feeding on blood and flea dirt, which is the digested blood from adult fleas. Yeah. Yuck. When they become pupa, they form cocoons and can wait a few days, or a year, until a host appears. They can nestle onto your dog or in your couch or carpet until they become adults, and then the cycle repeats itself. You may feel itchy just reading this. I'm itchy writing it.

However, if you happen to have an infestation of fleas, you will need to wash all bedding and dog beds, probably have your carpets cleaned, and your house sprayed. Your veterinarian can prescribe medicines, collars, or shampoos to help your coonhound get rid of his fleas. If your coonhound is on Advantage Multi® then he will be protected from fleas as well as round-worms, hookworms, whipworms, and sarcoptes mites.

Ticks

As long as I live, I'll never understand why God made ticks. They have got to be the nastiest, most disgusting arachnids there are. I hate spiders, too, don't get me wrong. Like spiders, ticks are basically worldwide, with the exception of Antarctica. There are 900 species of ticks! Tick fossils, preserved in amber, from *Deinocroton draculi* (does Dracula ring a bell?) have been discovered with dinosaur feathers dating back 99 million years. Great.

These nasty little blood-sucking parasites can detect an animal's breath, body odor, body heat, moisture, and vibrations. When a host is detected, most often by the smell of butyric acid emitted in sweat by warm-blooded creatures, they use two of their eight legs, the front pair, to grasp onto whatever unfortunate, butyric-acid-secreting creature walks by the grass or leaves that these little monsters are on.

Once a tick latches onto its host, strictly a vertebrate, it bites into the skin and excretes an anticoagulant so the host blood doesn't clot. If they aren't removed, they remain on their host until they are engorged and fall off. Engorged ticks are really nasty. Some tick species have 1500 to 3000 proteins in their saliva. Some of these proteins contain anti-inflammatory properties so the tick can remain undetected on the host for eight to ten days! The only benefit that I can see with ticks is that researchers are studying these proteins, called evasins, to develop drugs to help prevent heart attacks and strokes.

And if all of this information isn't frightening enough, just wait. There's more. Ticks are the vectors (carriers) of many diseases and infections. The most notable diseases are Lyme Disease, Rocky Mountain Spotted Fever, Ehrlichiosis, and Typhus. The bite from the Lone Star Tick can also cause allergic reactions to red meat.

Of course the best way to keep ticks from getting on you and your Treeing Walker Coonhound is to spray yourselves with tick repellent. Your veterinarian can also prescribe a tick collar or a monthly

HELPFUL TIP
Choosing a Brush

Tree Walker Coonhounds have short, dense coats that repel dirt and mud, making them excellent hunting companions. Grooming for these dogs is low maintenance and should include weekly brushing to remove dirt and loose hair. A hound glove, a rubberized glove with short rubber bristles, is a popular choice for grooming this type of coat. These gloves help improve the luster of your dog's coat, as well as remove excess fur.

chewable, such as Trifexis®, Bravecto®, or Simparica®, that repels ticks. You can also get Frontline® which is a between-the-shoulders liquid medication that prevents ticks from staying on your coonhound.

Don't let the fear of ticks keep you and your coonhound from enjoying the great outdoors. Use repellents and always check for ticks when you get home. Be sure you check between the toes and foot pads of your coonhound as well as his ears. Another place for ticks to invade is the gums. They can get anywhere! Even if you don't find a tick after your romp through the woods, check your coonhound the next day. Sometimes very tiny ticks, "seed ticks," might not be discovered, especially if your coonhound has lots of little black spots or a black saddle. You might discover these ticks a day or two later.

Tick Removal

Should you discover a tick on your Treeing Walker Coonhound, put on surgical gloves if you have them. You can soak the tick with alcohol or even peppermint oil. When it starts to loosen, grab it with a pair of tweezers or forceps. Try to not crush the tick as that can cause exposure to diseases that the tick may be carrying. Be sure that you have pulled the head out, too. If the head remains in the skin, it can cause disease. You can drop the tick in a jar of alcohol. Wash your hands thoroughly and you may need to disinfect the area on your coonhound where you removed the tick. There are also "tick keys" that can be used which look like bottle cap openers. These tick keys will remove all of the tick, including the head, quickly and efficiently. It might be a good idea to keep one of these in your pocket or attached to the leash when you and your coonhound explore and enjoy the outdoors.

Spay and Neuter Please!

Unless you plan on showing and breeding your Treeing Walker Coonhound, have your hound spayed or neutered as soon as possible. The old wives' tale that your hound will get fat if it gets "fixed" is simply not true. Your hound will get fat if you feed him extra food and he doesn't get proper exercise. The lack of a uterus or testicles does not contribute to weight gain.

Treeing Walker Coonhound puppies are absolutely adorable. That has been discussed. Puppies that are half Treeing Walker Coonhound will also be adorable. But they are preventable. Even if you have good intentions, accidents can happen. Fence jumpers can happen and that gorgeous female Treeing Walker Coonhound of yours could possibly have half-coonhound, half-whatever puppies in a couple of months.

Most veterinarians will spay or neuter dogs at six months of age. Some will do it sooner. Females may take a little longer to recover since their incision will be much bigger than a male who has been neutered. However, most dogs rebound easily, without much discomfort, from being spayed or neutered.

My friend Courtney fostered a pit bull who was discovered tied to a porch, pregnant and about to give birth. On Easter Sunday she had 13 puppies! At six week of age, the rescue organization came and got the puppies and had them spayed and neutered. I went to play with the puppies and they were romping around and playing when they came home from the vet like nothing had happened to them.

Rescue organizations want to insure that the dogs they adopt out don't reproduce, thereby keeping the rescues in business constantly. So if they are adopting out puppies, they might not be able to depend upon the adoptive family to follow through and spay/neuter their dogs. Spaying and neutering young puppies does carry risks, but it is one less thing the rescuers have to contend with if they know their puppies can't reproduce. And it saves the adoptive family some time and money later, too.

Female dogs go into their heat cycle twice per year. Therefore, they can have two litters of puppies each year. If an average litter is six puppies, that is twelve puppies per year for each female. Should the female continue to reproduce until she is ten years old, she will have had, on average, 120 puppies who can also reproduce. Intact males can impregnate hundreds and hundreds of females so they could potentially sire thousands of puppies. Many of these dogs will end up being euthanized in an animal shelter. They are perfectly good dogs, but might be unwanted and unloved.

There will never be a shortage of dogs so my advice is to spay or neuter your Treeing Walker Coonhound. When you fall in love with your Treeing Walker Coonhound, and possibly decide that you want to become a breeder, you can purchase another coonhound from a reputable breeder. For now, just assume that you don't want puppies and get your coonhound fixed.

Illness and Disease

Treeing Walker Coonhounds are basically very healthy dogs. Although all dogs can get sick on occasion, such as upset stomachs and diarrhea, for the most part, your coonhound should enjoy good health. Proper diet and exercise should help your coonhound enjoy a long and happy life.

However, you will want to monitor your Treeing Walker Coonhound for any signs of illness or discomfort. I have listed some common dog ailments

Photo Courtesy of
Jennifer Blankenship

that can affect all dogs, including your coonhound. Check your coonhound for signs of these illnesses.

Hip Dysplasia

Hip dysplasia may be considered the most common problem that Treeing Walker Coonhounds can have. Some breeds, such as golden retrievers and German shepherds, are definitely more susceptible to hip dysplasia, but it does occur in Treeing Walker Coonhounds. Of 800 coonhounds x-rayed for hip dysplasia by the Orthopedic Foundation of America, 15-21% were confirmed to have it. Hip dysplasia is inherited, thereby it can be bred into generations of dogs. Although puppies are not born with it, they may develop it as they mature. Hip dysplasia causes soreness and stiffness in the hind legs. The hips slip out of place, out of the hip sockets in the pelvis, possibly leading to arthritis. Note that your coonhound could also experience elbow dysplasia, too. Keep your Treeing Walker Coonhound on the lighter side to keep extra weight off his hips. Calcium supplements can interfere with bone and cartilage development so avoid giving your coonhound calcium supplements. Strenuous exercise can affect the hips. If you hunt with your coonhound, know that prolonged standing on his hind legs treeing raccoons might potentially affect his hips. Putting your coonhound on a supplement such as glucosamine might prevent hip and joint issues. As noted in Chapter 4, the AKC recommends that Treeing Walker Coonhound breeders conduct hip evaluations for their puppies and older dogs. If you are getting your coonhound from a breeder, make sure that they have checked your coonhound's hips. You will also want a health guarantee from the breeder.

Eye Anomalies

Eye anomalies can occur in Treeing Walker Coonhounds. Again, all dogs can suffer from eye diseases and as your coonhound ages, he might develop cataracts. Injuries to the eyes can always occur, especially if your dog hunts and ends up fighting with a raccoon or running through brush and brambles. The AKC recommends that breeders have their Treeing Walker Coonhounds evaluated by a canine ophthalmologist, as noted in Chapter 4.

Bowie had a cherry eye, which is common in dogs and is the result of the prolapse of the nictitating membrane, or "third eyelid" in dogs. The nictitating membrane is a protective layer and has a gland which produces the protective tear film for the eye, which keeps your coonhound from developing dry eyes. Cherry eye occurs when this gland pops out. Your veterinarian can remove the cherry eye and your coonhound should have a very good recovery.

Dogs can have ectropion, or droopy lower eyelids. Some breeds, particularly hounds such as bloodhounds and Basset hounds have ectropion and it is almost considered "normal" and may even be considered a desirable characteristic ("sad eyes") when breeding dogs. It really isn't a desirable trait. Should your Treeing Walker Coonhound develop ectropion, have him checked by your veterinarian. The droopiness of the lower eyelid can eventually cause conjunctivitis, an inflammation of the conjunctiva. The conjunctiva is a clear tissue that covers the sclera (white part of the eye) and the inner eyelids. Surgery may be required depending upon the severity of the droopiness.

Entropion is more painful as the eyelids turn inward. As a result of this, the eye balls and the cornea, which covers the eye, are constantly irritated by the eyelashes and hairs rubbing against them. Prolonged irritation can lead to ulcers in the cornea and scarring, which can affect your hound's vision. Entropion can occur on the upper and lower eyelids, in one eye, or in both eyes. If you notice your coonhound consistently blinking, squinting or rubbing his eyes, or notice redness and swelling of the eyes, have your veterinarian check your coonhound's eyes as soon as possible. Mild cases may only require treatment with antibiotics while more severe cases will require surgery.

Thyroid Conditions

Thyroid conditions, while treatable, are common in dogs. As referenced in Chapter 4, the AKC recommends that breeders have their Treeing Walker Coonhounds' thyroids evaluated. The thyroid gland, located in your coonhound's throat, produces hormones that are important in metabolism.

Hypothyroidism occurs when the thyroid gland does not produce enough of the hormones, such as thyroxine. Your coonhound might begin to gain weight (when on a regular feed and exercise schedule) feel lethargic, have changes in the coat (excessive shedding and hair loss) or skin (thickening), be reluctant to exercise or not feel like exercising as much, be intolerant to colder temperatures, not be as sharp mentally, and even have reproductive issues if your coonhound is intact. Your veterinarian will conduct a blood test to determine the levels of thyroxine in your coonhound. If the levels are below normal, your coonhound will get a prescription for thyroxine and have his thyroxine levels checked periodically. This will potentially turn into a lifelong medication. About 16% of coonhounds will be diagnosed with hypo-thyroidism according to the Michigan State University Thyroid Database.

Hyperthyroidism is the result of your coonhound producing too much thyroxine, causing the metabolism to work overtime. Thyroid cancer is the primary cause. Your coonhound will lose weight, be hyperexcitable, have an increased appetite as well as thirst, increased urination and amounts of stool, may have vomiting and diarrhea, and heart problems. Medications to help with the abundance of thyroid hormones can be prescribed. If your coonhound has thyroid cancer, your veterinarian will discuss options, such as surgery, chemotherapy, or radiation treatments.

Cushing's Disease

Cushing's Disease results from a tumor in the pituitary gland, which is located at the base of the brain. Cushing's Disease is common in bea-gles, but it would behoove you to be aware of it as the owner of a Treeing Walker Coonhound. Excess cortisol, the stress hormone, is released, causing extreme thirst and excessive urination. Hair loss and skin lesions, thinning of the skin, obesity and lack of energy are symptoms. Many times, Cushing's Disease may not be diagnosed quickly as it may take time for the symptoms to appear and the symptoms might be associated with your coonhound sim-ply getting older. Prolonged use of prednisone or dexamethasone can cause Cushing's Disease, but may stop when the steroid use is stopped. Diagnosing Cushing's Disease is conducted through time-consuming blood and urine tests along with administering hormones or steroids and then testing the blood again after several hours to determine cortisol levels. Treatment depends upon the location of the tumor and surgery to remove the tumor can be complicated. Once a dog is diagnosed with Cushing's Disease, life expectancy is about two years.

Bloat

Bloat is a very serious and deadly condition that your Treeing Walker Coonhound can develop. Gastric dilatation-volvulus (GDV), or bloat, consti-tutes a veterinary emergency. During bloat, the stomach fills with air (gastric dilatation), and then twists (volvulus), increasing the pressure and prevent-ing the blood from the hind legs and abdomen to flow to the heart. Blood begins to pool in the hind end, which reduces the working blood volume. Your coonhound will go into shock. When the stomach flips, this cuts off blood flow to the pancreas and spleen. The pancreas then begins producing toxic hormones which can stop the heart. Dogs who are experiencing bloat will begin retching and their abdomens will enlarge. It will be painful for the dog if you press on his belly. Your coonhound can go into shock within two hours so it is imperative that you get him to the veterinarian as soon as possible. Your veterinarian will treat the shock first, and then surgery will be required to untwist the stomach. It should be noted that 90% of dogs who experience bloat and survive will more than likely get bloat again. Deep, narrow-chested, tall dogs (coonhounds) and very large breeds, such as Great Danes or St. Bernards, are more susceptible to bloat. Males are more at-risk than females and spaying/neutering has no effect on the risk of bloat. Bloat can occur if the parents or other relatives experience it, so these dogs should be spayed or neutered. The causes of bloat are unknown and prevention is sketchy at best. Soybean meal, oils, and fats listed as the first four ingredients of dog food increase the chance of bloat. Feeding your coonhound a meal in the morning and evening, helping him slow down to eat if he gobbles up his food at record speed, reducing stress and anxiety, and keeping your Treeing Walker Coonhound happy may help decrease the chance of him experiencing bloat.

Cancer

Cancer can affect all dogs. Treeing Walker Coonhounds are not at risk any more than another dog is. Cancer just happens. It happened to my sweet Casey. But since I don't know what happened to him the first six years of his life, I can't say for sure why he got cancer; if it was exposure or injury or what. Cancer just sucks.

So now you know of some very serious and also common medical issues that can happen to your coonhound. They are things that you need to be aware of and know about. Don't be afraid that your Treeing Walker Coonhound will contract any of these conditions. He may. He may not. Chances are, with the wonderful care you give him, he will be fine and have a happy, healthy life. Don't let the worry and fear of these illnesses keep you from getting a Treeing Walker Coonhound. Get one! Enjoy him!

CHAPTER 13

Food and Dietary Needs for Your Treeing Walker Coonhound

Food for Your Treeing Walker Coonhound

Coonhounds in general, and Treeing Walker Coonhounds are no exception, will eat just about anything. As a general rule, coonhounds are not picky eaters. If it is in their bowl, chances are, it will be eaten.

Expensive dog food doesn't mean that it is better than "ordinary" dog food. Check around with your friends and see what they feed their dogs. If you got your coonhound from a breeder, see what they feed their dogs. Your veterinarian will also be able to recommend a healthy dog food for your Treeing Walker Coonhound. If your coonhound develops allergies, check with your veterinarian. Salmon and sweet potato grain-free kibble may be a good choice.

You will also need to decide if you want to serve wet, canned dog food or dry kibble. This basically comes down to your preference of picking up wet, runny poop or dry, compact poop. I opt for a high-quality kibble that is not cheap, but also doesn't require a second mortgage on the house. Feed according to the guidelines. Your Treeing Walker Coonhound won't agree with the guidelines.

If your Treeing Walker Coonhound is an "easy keeper" and doesn't get tons of exercise, you might consider feeding a little bit less, or feeding smaller portions in the morning and evening. Trust me. Your coonhound will not mind eating two times per day. If weight gain is a problem, add some green beans into the food. They are a healthy filler without a lot of calories. Please try to make time to take your Treeing Walker Coonhound for a walk, too.

Photo Courtesy of
Ann Jayne

HELPFUL TIP
TWCs and Children

Treeing Walker Coonhounds are typically gentle and affectionate dogs, making them a good choice for families with children. Because of their high energy level, these dogs are best suited for an active family that can give their dog around 60 minutes of activity every day. TWCs have a very high prey drive, so they should always be walked on a leash and never by a child who is too young to control the dog. As a rule, children should be at least 10 years old before they are allowed to walk a dog without assistance. This prey drive also means that TWCs may not be a good choice for a household with small pets such as hamsters, rabbits, or mice.

Check with your veterinarian about supplements, too. If your Treeing Walker Coonhound starts to get arthritic, you will need a joint-care supplement. Also, you might want to consider fish oil for his coat.

Find healthy snacks for your hound, too. Your Treeing Walker Coonhound will begin to "train you" in the business of rewarding him with a snack every time he asks to go outside. Or asks to come inside. Pees outside. Poops outside. Looks cute (all of the time). Walks by the treat jar. Wakes up from a nap. Thinks of any other reason on God's green earth why a treat is deserved. This is an easy trap to fall into and extremely difficult to climb out of and your Treeing Walker Coonhound will be persistent. That is as sure as death and taxes. I'm sorry to say that you will have to put your foot down and hold the line. Extra treats mean extra calories. Extra calories mean extra weight.

If the budget is tight, consider having your dog food shipped to your house, perhaps monthly or every-other-month on auto ship. Some stores and online businesses have reward programs. Buying in bulk or when your particular dog food is on sale is a way to save money, too.

On a final note, when choosing dog food, snacks, and rawhides or "chewies," make sure that they are made in America. That way, you can be relatively sure that there are not any toxic ingredients, such as lead, in the food or snack.

Home-Made Dog Food

You might also consider making your own dog food. Research it on the internet and find many nutritious recipes. Make sure that the recipe will meet the dietary needs for your coonhound, such as the amount of protein and healthy fats he needs for his skin, coat, brain, eyes, energy, and inner health.

*Photo Courtesy of
Nancy Vermaat*

Dangerous Foods for Your Treeing Walker Coonhound

I think it is okay to give your coonhound little bits and nibbles of some of the food you are eating. Just because your Treeing Walker Coonhound enjoys "people" food doesn't mean that all people food is healthy for him. There are foods that can be harmful to your Treeing Walker Coonhound, so avoid giving these foods to him. I have included a partial list, but you can research more harmful foods on the internet by searching for "toxic foods for dogs."

- Alcohol, found in alcoholic beverages, yeast and vanilla extract can cause canine bloat or the rupture of the intestines. A swollen stomach, seizures, vomiting, diarrhea, disorientation, coma, and death are possible.

- Avocado will destroy the heart and lungs. Ingestion of any part of the avocado can cause a swollen abdomen, difficulty in breathing, seizures, coma and death.

- Chocolate will be addressed separately.

- Caffeine can affect your Treeing Walker Coonhound the same way that chocolate can. Caffeine pills, coffee beans, and large amounts of coffee or tea should never be given to your coonhound. In addition to the symptoms chocolate induces, restlessness, weakness, panting, and convulsions can also occur.

- Grapes and raisins can be fatal when eaten by your coonhound. They can cause kidney damage, vomiting, diarrhea, decreased urine production, weakness, and a drunken gait.

- Onions cause hemolytic anemia, which destroys red blood cells. Your coonhound can have pale gums, a rapid heart rate, weakness, lethargy, vomiting, and diarrhea.

- Macadamia nuts are generally not fatal to your Treeing Walker Coonhound, but they can make your coonhound severely ill within an elevated heart rate and body temperature, weakness, depression, muscle stiffness, tremors and vomiting with 6 hours after ingestion.

- Xylitol, which is an artificial sweetener, causes your coonhound's pancreas to increase the output of insulin, resulting in low blood sugar. Xylitol can cause liver damage. Your coonhound will begin showing symptoms of weakness, a drunken gait, seizures, and collapsing within 30 minutes of ingesting gum or candy that contains xylitol.

Photo Courtesy of
David and Christine Gyza

- Chicken and turkey bones are soft and brittle. It is easy for them to splinter, which can cause tears in your coonhound's esophagus, stomach, and intestines. This damage can be severe and even life-threatening. A friend of mine is a veterinarian and she said that the minimum for extracting bones or repairing tears is $1200.00. Yes, wolves, coyotes, and foxes eat chickens, and thus, their bones. Your Treeing Walker Coonhound is not a wolf, coyote, or fox, so please don't give him chicken bones. Pork chop bones have sharp tips, too, so avoid giving your coonhound these bones, too. Likewise, small round beef or ham bones can get caught in your coonhound's teeth, the roof of his mouth, or stuck in his throat. Avoid these types of bones as well.

With regard to chocolate and the dangers it presents to your hound, know that chocolate contains theobromine, which is similar to caffeine and affects the central nervous system as well as the heart, lungs, and kidneys. Your Treeing Walker Coonhound cannot metabolize a large amount of chocolate and may begin vomiting, have diarrhea, seizures, or muscle tremors, become hyperactive, or suffer cardiac arrest.

This doesn't mean that if your hound eats one M&M® that he will suddenly go into convulsions and die. The amount of chocolate ingested, in conjunction with your dog's weight, is what can cause the ill effects. Obviously small breeds of dogs, or your Treeing Walker Coonhound puppy, cannot ingest large amounts of chocolate.

Milk chocolate is not as harmful as dark chocolate or baking chocolate. However, the signs of ingesting chocolate, regardless of the type, are the same. If your coonhound is experiencing mild signs of chocolate toxicity, whether it is milk chocolate, dark chocolate, or baking chocolate (which is stronger and more toxic), he may begin vomiting, have diarrhea or be hyperexcitable. Moderate signs are tremors and heart irregularities and severe signs involve your hound having seizures. Signs of chocolate toxicity should begin appearing within six hours.

Mild signs should not be taken lightly and it would be a good idea to consult your veterinarian if you know that your coonhound has treated himself to some chocolate. Be sure and tell your vet what kind of chocolate your hound ate as the amount of theobromine varies in different chocolate products. Cocoa powder is the most toxic.

To be safe, just don't give your dog any chocolate. Remember that your Treeing Walker Coonhound might be a counter-surfer so keep all chocolate products pushed way back or even in a drawer or high cabinet. I personally don't think an M&M® here or there is a big deal, but it does start a bad habit and probably a lifelong preference for chocolate.

Sometimes "happy" accidents happen, as was the case with my sister. Her miniature dachshund, Lucky, got into her purse and devoured two or three mini candy bars. Not only did Lucky get them out of her purse, he managed to chew open the wrappers and get the candy bars out and ate them as a reward for his hard work. Lucky was fine, but my sister had to make sure to keep her purse in a place where her nosy dachshund choco-holic couldn't get to it.

Here is a simple breakdown for amounts of chocolate your dog can eat and start exhibiting symptoms, including the size of the dog (puppy) and type of chocolate:

Small dogs (6-19 pounds)

- Milk chocolate: mild signs 30-50 grams, moderate signs 60-100 grams, severe signs 90-150 grams
- Dark chocolate: mild signs 12-20 grams, moderate signs 24-40 grams, severe signs 36-60 grams
- Baking chocolate: mild signs 4-7 grams, moderate signs 8-13 grams, severe signs 12-20 grams

Medium dogs (20-40 pounds)

- Milk chocolate: mild signs 100-150 grams, moderate signs 200-300 grams, severe signs 300-450 grams
- Dark chocolate: mild signs 40-60 grams, moderate signs 80-120 grams, severe signs 120-180 grams
- Baking chocolate: mild signs 13-20 grams, moderate signs 25-40 grams, severe signs 40-60 grams

Large dogs (50+ pounds)

- Milk chocolate: mild signs 300+ grams, moderate signs 600+ grams, severe signs 900+ grams
- Dark chocolate: mild signs 120+ grams, moderate signs 240+ grams, severe signs 360+ grams
- Baking chocolate: mild signs 40+ grams, moderate signs 80+ grams, severe signs 120+ grams

If you never give your Treeing Walker Coonhound "people" food, then you won't have to worry about toxic foods, unless he gets into the trash. If you decide to let him sample what you are eating, make sure it is safe for him. Chances are one chocolate chip or a little avocado on a bite of hamburger meat isn't going to kill your coonhound. Be smart about what you feed him, whether it is people or dog food, and your hound should be just fine.

CHAPTER 14

Show Dogs Or Hunting Dogs

Your Treeing Walker Coonhound might just open up the world of dog shows and coonhound trials to you. If you are a hunter, you might just simply enjoy taking your coonhound out for a romp in the woods or perhaps tree some raccoons. This might evolve into entering coonhound hunting trials. If you decide to keep it on the quieter side of dog shows, then you can enter dog shows based on conformation (bench shows), whether they are AKC- or UKC-sanctioned, or a low-key local dog show.

AKC Competitions

If your AKC Treeing Walker Coonhound puppy or grown dog has AKC papers, he can compete in standard conformation dog shows, coonhound hunting events, or both.

The AKC offers a variety of competitions that your registered Treeing Walker Coonhound can enter. If you know that your hound has very good conformation (everything is in proportion to the AKC standards for the Treeing Walker Coonhound), and the breeder will have informed you of this when you got your puppy, then you might consider showing him against other Treeing Walker Coonhounds.

Conformation guidelines and specifications for any breed are set in order to keep the "best" attributes and traits for breeding purposes, to keep the finest and purest bloodlines going. The coonhound who best meets the conformation guidelines wins. (Of course, everyone's dog is the best, whether he is a show dog or not.) But to continue the uniqueness and character of the breed to future generations, and to weed out undesirable traits, defects and deformities, the dogs who are deemed to be the most in line with AKC's standards will win the shows. In fact, defects and deformities are usually automatic disqualifications. To maintain the integrity of the Treeing Walker Coonhound breed, preventing the passing on of less-than-desirable traits should be prevented. You may have the sweetest Treeing Walker

Photo Courtesy of
Tia Schmelzer

FUN FACT
Dock-Jumping Record

A Treeing Walker Coonhound/Doberman mix named Bo Nose smashed the dock-jumping record in 2017 by jumping 27 feet at the Purina Pro Plan Incredible Dog Challenge. The previous record was 25 feet, and the current record as of 2020 is 36 feet, 2 inches. Bo Nose's owner, Crystal McClaran, is the owner of the nonprofit rescue "Bo Nose Rescue," based in Florida.

Coonhound that ever lived, but if he has health issues that were passed down from one or both of his parents, and he could pass them on to his own offspring, he needs to be neutered. Females with genetic defects should be spayed. These dogs will make fine pets, just not show dogs.

If you are interested in showing your registered Treeing Walker Coonhound, the AKC sponsors clinics and workshops so you can educate yourself first-hand regarding the dog show world. You can also contact the breeder where you purchased your coonhound (if they show coonhounds) for advice and possibly training, as well as professional dog trainers to help you train and prepare your coonhound, and you, for the dog shows.

AKC dog show events for your Treeing Walker Coonhound include the general showmanship show, junior showmanship, puppy shows, and actual coonhound event shows.

During showmanship dog shows, your hound is presented, shown and ranked according to his conformation and movement. He will need to learn how to stand still while the judge examines him and trot around the arena with you or the handler so the judge can observe his gait and expression. Keep in mind that this is not a "beauty pageant" for coonhounds (although they are indeed beautiful dogs). Again, it is to ensure that the best genes, traits, and characteristics are being represented. If it is a breed-specific show, your Treeing Walker Coonhound will only compete against other Treeing Walker Coonhounds. During larger shows, he will compete against other Treeing Walker Coonhounds, then the winner will compete against the other winners of other hound groups, like beagles, blueticks, redbones, and Afghan hounds, to name a few. In larger shows, including the Westminster Kennel Club Dog Show (the Kentucky Derby of dog shows),the winner of the Hound Group proceeds to the Best in Show class where he will compete with the winners of the other groups: Herding, Non-Sporting, Sporting, Terrier, Toy, and Working.

If you have an AKC-registered Treeing Walker Coonhound puppy that is between four to six months old, you can enter him in AKC 4-6 Month

Beginner Puppy Competition classes. Although there are no championships awarded at these shows, puppy shows are an excellent way to socialize your puppy and get him ready for the larger shows. Your coonhound puppy can earn points as he wins. Once he earns 10 points, he earns his Puppy of Achievement and at 15 points, he will get a Certificate of Merit. Note that professional handlers are not allowed to show your puppy or any other puppies for that matter. Once you decide you want to show your Treeing Walker Coonhound puppy, find an event (the AKC website will have a list of events), contact the show secretary and you will receive an entry form and the list of rules and requirements.

AKC Junior Showmanship classes are available for kids ages nine to eighteen who would like to show dogs. They learn how to present and handle their Treeing Walker Coonhounds (skills that are needed later in more advanced dog shows) as well as good sportsmanship. In addition, your Treeing Walker Coonhound will enjoy these shows and get extra attention and socialization as he begins his show career.

The AKC also sponsors the AKC Raccoon Hound Events Program. Events include Nite Hunts, Hunt Tests, Field Trials, Water Races, and Bench Shows. So if you decide that you want to hunt with your Treeing Walker Coonhound, and he has AKC papers, not only can you show him in conformation shows, but also in events to show off his raccoon-treeing skills, even chasing his prey (native game depending upon the area) through naturally-occurring waters and land. Your Treeing Walker Coonhound has the potential to earn championship titles in conformation and hunting trials as he is one of seven breeds allowed to compete in the Raccoon Hound Events. Go to www.akc. org/sports/field-events-hounds/coonhounds/ to find more information.

Agility Trials

Agility competitions are available for any breed of registered dog, unregistered dog, mixed breed dog, intact dog, or spayed/neutered dogs.

During agility competitions, your Treeing Walker Coonhound will have an established course that he must complete within a desired time. There will 14-20 obstacles, such as weave poles, jumps, seesaws, tunnels, and pause tables (your coonhound will need to stop and pause here) comprising the course. They must be followed in a specific order, which you will memorize and then cue and guide your hound through during the event. So this event is as much for you as it is for your coonhound! And you will need to run around the course with him, showing and telling him what is next.

The AKC offers seminars on agility courses and it would be very wise to attend some of these before you and your Treeing Walker Coonhound begin your agility career. It would also benefit you to watch some agility trials. They are fun to watch whether you ever plan to compete with your coonhound or not.

Agility competitions within the AKC are open to unregistered dogs or mixed-breed dogs. However, unregistered dogs may be registered through the AKC Indefinite Listing Privilege (ILP) and mixed-breed dogs can be registered through the Canine Partners Program. The AKC offers breed-specific agility trials as well as group trials (herding, working, hound, etc.).

Your Treeing Walker Coonhound will need to be at least 15 months old and he should have a higher level of energy and enthusiasm so he can compete at his best and possibly set the record for the fastest time for the course. He will need to get along with other dogs as well, since there will be many dogs in the events. This usually isn't a problem with coonhounds since they are used to hunting in packs. Listening to your commands and obedience training will be crucial for your coonhound before you even consider competing in agility events.

Perhaps your Treeing Walker Coonhound is a rescue dog. While you could enter him in the AKC trials through the Canine Partners Program, there are also agility competitions that specifically promote rescued and adopted dogs.

There are rules and standards that apply to the agility course equipment. You can purchase your own equipment (it is not cheap) or build your own equipment. If you decide to build your own jumps and bridges and seesaws, note that you should build them according to the specifics outlined in the Regulations for Agility.

Additionally, and this is where observing agility competitions first will help you, there are certain ways your coonhound needs to navigate around the obstacles. For instance, with the weave poles, your coonhound will need to enter the weave poles leading with his left shoulder. Likewise, on the seesaw or a bridge, his feet must touch the yellow portion of the bridge at the end before he takes off for the next obstacle.

You can research agility trials and obstacles on the internet or through books and videos. A great place to start is https://www.akc.org/sports/agility/getting-started/.

Although Treeing Walker Coonhounds are not necessarily the dog one might think of initially for agility, these hounds are agile and fast, so there is no reason to think that your exuberant floppy-eared friend won't thrive as an agility dog. It will provide hours of bonding and fun for you and your hound, whether you are seeking blue ribbons and trophies or not.

Photo Courtesy of
Nicole Cameron

Hunting

I am not a hunter. Not at all. But after we had to pay a ton of money to get rid of raccoons in our attic, clean out the attic, and get new insulation (insurance won't pay for raccoon damage, even if the masked critters chew through electrical wires and burn down your house), I began to re-evaluate raccoon hunting. I think it just might be an absolute blast to go on a raccoon hunt and watch Treeing Walker Coonhounds, the "people's choice" of coonhound breeds, in action. In their element. Doing what they were bred to do.

If you have never been on a raccoon hunt, much less with your coonhound, it would greatly benefit you to find an experienced coon hunter and learn from him or her. Go on coon hunts with them. Get first-hand experience and see if coon hunting is for you. You can also watch coonhound hunts on YouTube. Be aware that it may take up to two years to get your Treeing Walker Coonhound properly trained as a hunting dog. Sometimes, it may take less time.

Coon hunting happens at night, when raccoons are most active. There may be a pack of coonhounds and hunters, or just a couple. Equipment to hunt raccoons is minimal: a .22 rifle (and normally only one person carries a rifle) and a headlamp since humans can't see in the dark. Proper clothing for the woods and weather is a must.

Of course, in the 21st Century, coonhound hunting has evolved. Rather than spend days hunting for a coonhound that excitedly ran off, hunters can outfit their hounds with GPS tracking collars to locate them. Some collars are even advanced enough to record and transmit the dog's habits, such as if he is on the move, has stopped moving, or is maybe barking at another treed racoon. Your Treeing Walker Coonhound can be trained to stay at the tree until you arrive so you don't have to worry about him running off. But a GPS collar wouldn't be a bad investment just in case your coonhound sees another raccoon on the ground and takes off after *Procyon lotor* in a frenzied moment.

Note that not all hunters will shoot the raccoons. Some hunt strictly for the thrill of treeing a raccoon, then moving on to find another one to tree. Others hunt for raccoon meat (no thanks) and pelts. Many hunt just to hear the beautiful songs that only coonhounds can sing.

Photo Courtesy of
Matt Michael

Coonhound Hunting Trials

There are also non-AKC coonhound hunting trials. The United Kennel Club (UKC) hosts coonhound hunting trials and most states, usually in the south and eastern states, sponsor coonhound hunting trials.

If you have ever read Where the Red Fern Grows by Wilson Rawls, then you might be interested in the Red Fern Festival in eastern Oklahoma. During the last week of April, this event hosts the Hound Dog Field Trials in Tahlequah, Oklahoma. Although the dogs in Where the Red Fern Grows were Redbone Coonhounds, Treeing Walker Coonhounds, along with Blueticks, Black and Tan Coonhounds, Plott Hounds, American English Coonhounds (Redticks) and Catahoula Leopard Hounds are welcome to participate.

Discover and research what events interest you. There will be entry fees and possibly membership fees as well as rules and guidelines. Breed standards will be outlined, specifically for UKC and AKC events, including disqualifications for blind or deaf dogs, dogs having cryptorchids, or wrong colorations, including albinos. Dogs who proudly sport scars from hunts as well as bitches who have nursed several litters and have dropped udders will not be disqualified.

Points are scored for treeing raccoons, being the first hound to tree a raccoon, or catching the raccoon. Points will be deducted if no raccoon is seen or the hound leaves the tree or gets into a fight with other dogs. There are other descriptions for accumulating and deducting points and you can find them at https://www.ukcdogs.com/docs/rulebooks/2020-coon-hound-rulebook.pdf or whatever hunt you decide to enter.

The highest number of points leads to trophies, plaques and even cash prizes, awarded at the end of the trial. Don't forget that you earn your bragging rights and get to spend quality time with many of these glorious hounds!

The Coondog Cemetery

Tucked away in Cherokee, Alabama is the Key Underwood Coon Dog Memorial Cemetery. This cemetery, located at 4945 Coondog Cemetery Road was founded on September 4, 1937 in honor of a coon dog named Troop. Key Underwood and Troop met regularly in hunting camps for 15 years to hunt raccoons. When Troop, considered the best hunting dog around at the time, passed away, Underwood knew that the only place that Troop could be laid to rest was at their hunting camp in the Freedom Hills near Tuscumbia, AL.

Troop's body was placed in a cotton pick sack and placed three feet in the ground. A simple chimney brick was his grave marker. Underwood chiseled Troop's name and the date of Troop's death into the brick with a hammer and screwdriver. Today, a special marker has been placed over Troop's grave. More than 300 coon dogs have been buried in this special cemetery.

But not just any dog can be buried here. Owners must claim that their dog is indeed an authentic coon dog and this must be verified by a witness. Staff at the cemetery must view the dog and declare it a true hunting coon dog.

Gravestones range from the simple (wooden or brick grave markers) to elaborate (engraved and elaborate granite markers). The gravestones may include the details about the dog, including championships earned (and there are National Champions from the AKC and UKC buried here), the owner's name, brass plates, reliefs of hounds and raccoons, and coonhounds sleeping on top of the gravestones. Some graves are outlines with bricks or rocks. Special mementos such as food bowls and collars are placed at the graves. Funerals for coonhounds have been recorded and you can watch some of them on YouTube.

The cemetery is open to the public and every Labor Day, there is a special celebration honoring the dogs. American flags are placed on the graves. Bands, lots of food and storytelling ("liars contest") are part of the festivities.

Who knows? You might be the owner of the next Champion Treeing Walker Coonhound and decide to lay your friend to rest at the Key Underwood Coon Dog Memorial Cemetery someday.

CHAPTER 15
Senior Citizens

Life Span

As was noted in Chapter 1, your Treeing Walker Coonhound has an average life span of fifteen years. Once he turns seven or eight, he will be considered middle age and he might, or might not, begin slowing down a bit. And as was noted in Chapter 6, your coonhound will age faster than you as he has to cram many years into a few. He might start showing signs of age at eight or nine years of age, but for ease, we will call him a senior at 10 years old. By the time he is 12 or 13, he will be considered geriatric.

Photo Courtesy of Amanda Brimmer

Food and Supplements for Your Aging
Treeing Walker Coonhound

When your hound approaches middle age, it would be wise for you to start noticing any issues that might start affecting him. It would also be a good time to start him on a joint supplement, containing glucosamine and possibly MSM. CBD oil might be an option, too. Dogs cannot process THC, found in marijuana, so don't give him anything with THC in it. Although Bowie is only five years old, I started him on a joint supplement as he was limping occasionally. I don't know if it was just because he had slept 12 hours on the same side or what. But after losing Casey to cancer, which started by him limping, I didn't want to take any

HELPFUL TIP
Dealing with
Ear Infections

Tree Walker Coonhounds are an overall healthy breed, but because of their long ears, they can be prone to developing ear infections. Early signs of ear infections in dogs can be subtle and include whining, headshaking, and scratching the affected ear. Later signs can include discharge, a smell, redness of the ear canal, and crusting/scabs in the ear. Canine ear infections are treated with a medicated cleaning solution administered by your vet, and home care may include special cleaning instructions and, sometimes, antibiotics. Be sure to check your dog's ears weekly, clean them when needed, and keep them dry to prevent the growth of bacteria.

chances. Since Bowie has been on the supplement his veterinarian recommended, I have not seen him limp. I take joint supplements and I give them to my horse, too, who is 27.

Regarding his diet, your Treeing Walker Coonhound should be able to stay on his regular dog food unless he develops problems. However, if he gets really old, or develops dental issues, you will need to check with your veterinarian and possibly change from a dry kibble to perhaps a soft food and maybe determine if he needs more or less protein. If you notice your hound losing weight and you are feeding him his usual meals, you will need to have your veterinarian look at him. Likewise, as your coonhound ages and his activities slow down, he might begin to gain weight. Again, have your veterinarian recommend a food that is appropriate for your aging coonhound. Excess treats mean excess calories, too, so you might have to restrict his intake of treats. Ensuring that your Treeing Walker Coonhound stays properly hydrated is crucial, too.

Health Issues

In Chapter 12, you were made aware of a few illnesses and diseases that can affect your Treeing Walker Coonhound at basically any age. So while he could develop these as he gets older, he might not. But there are age-related issues that could affect your coonhound. You should have him examined by your veterinarian if he begins showing any signs of the following:

Photo Courtesy of Rebecca Reeves

Photo Courtesy of
John and Tammy Wellman

- Arthritis might just be the number one issue that an aging dog will face. If your coonhound yelps as he walks or perhaps when you pet him in a certain place, he might be developing arthritis.

- Incontinence can affect your coonhound as he gets older. It may or may not be the result of a disease such as Cushing's Disease. It could just be the result of his bladder, intestines, and sphincter muscles being 15 years old.

- Chronic pain might not be the result of arthritis. It could stem from something else such as an autoimmune disease or simply the fact that your beloved Treeing Walker Coonhound is old.

- Blindness can affect your coonhound as he ages. While he might not become totally blind, his eyesight might diminish to the point that he bumps into things or doesn't see you until you are very near him.

- Deafness happens when his ears age with the rest of him. If he sleeps through, or flat out doesn't hear the rattling of the treat bag, he may be experiencing hearing loss.

- Cognitive decline might happen as your hound ages. His brain is aging, too, so he might not seem as sharp as he used to be or else he wanders aimlessly throughout the house. He might withdraw to himself more and more, too.

- Skin problems in the form of dryness, itchiness, redness and even bruising might begin to manifest as your hound ages. Cuts may take longer to heal and the skin may lose its elasticity.

Preparing Your House for Your Aging Treeing Walker Coonhound

Just as you had to prepare your house for your coonhound when he was a puppy, you may need to make some adjustments now that he's old. He will definitely need a soft but supportive dog bed in case he can no longer get on the couch or in the chair with you. If you still want him on your furniture, you might get a ramp or steps to help him have better access to your couch, chair or bed.

If incontinence becomes a problem and there is absolutely no way to hurry him outside to do his business, you might need to invest in some pee pads and place them throughout the house. Avoid scolding your friend. He can't help it and he knows that he isn't supposed to poop or pee in the house. Pet him and tell him it's okay. Invest in a good cleaner and don't worry about it. If you have nice carpet, you might get some cheap rugs at the thrift store and put them down on the carpet where your coonhound spends time. Expensive rugs should be rolled up and removed for the time being.

When Casey had cancer and had trouble walking on our hardwood floors and tile, I bought cheap yoga mats and made trails throughout the house. It helped him navigate and was soft on his feet. Again, you can probably find them at discount stores or even garage sales and thrift stores.

If your Treeing Walker Coonhound's eyesight is getting bad, you might mark any steps, especially if you have a sunken living room, with blue tape so he can see it. You might even put a small ramp there, too. Sometimes even a small step can be difficult for an aging or arthritic dog.

Activities for Your Older Treeing Walker Coonhound

Just because your Treeing Walker Coonhound is aging doesn't mean that you have to stop your activities with him. He will still enjoy walks with you; you just might have to make them shorter and more leisurely. He still might want to play with you but maybe his playtime is shorter now.

Photo Courtesy of Katie Harris

If he was a hunting dog, you can still take him on easy walks in the woods or park and let him sniff the trees or bark at squirrels. For his past agility days, he can still manage to walk through the weave poles or the tunnels. Praise him when he does this!

Favorite toys tucked in his bed might provide a source of comfort for your old buddy. He will always appreciate something with your smell on it, too.

Spend Time With Your Old Treeing Walker Coonhound

Even if your Treeing Walker Coonhound's active lifestyle is winding down, you still need to spend quality time with him. Sit outside with him. Take a walk around the yard with him. Let him get in your lap while you read or watch television. Make sure to pet him and talk to him.

Remind him of your past adventures and tell him how much you love him. While he might not hear well, chances are he can still smell you and he will always enjoy having your hands on him. He has given himself to you his whole life. Remember that you are his whole world. No time spent with your old friend will be wasted. Ever.

CHAPTER 16

Telling Your Treeing Walker Coonhound Good-bye

The Hardest Decision

Your coonhound can live to the ripe old age of 15, perhaps even longer. I know some people who had their coonhounds for as long as 18 years. Whether through natural causes, old age, illness, disease, or accidents, inevitably you will be faced with having to tell your beloved coonhound good-bye.

I hope that your Treeing Walker Coonhound is blessed with health and a long-life, giving you a chance to hug and kiss him and tell him good-bye before he slips away quietly and peacefully in your arms. I hope. Personally, I believe that our pets go to heaven. That helps keep me going; that I will see Casey again someday, along with my other pets.

For me, one of the hardest decisions I ever had to make was having my Casey put to sleep. He was diagnosed with cancer in his C-6 and C-7 vertebrae that began causing loss of muscle mass and very limited mobility. This happened very, very quickly. I wouldn't have made the decision except that Casey suddenly was unable to get up. He didn't pee, although he was drinking water. I knew

FUN FACT
Foundation Stock Service

The Foundation Stock Service (FSS) is a record-keeping service created by the AKC for experimental and nascent dog breeds. Many breeders seek to have their breeds fully recognized by the AKC by first registering with the FSS. Treeing Walker Coonhounds were recorded in the FSS from 1995 until they were officially recognized by the AKC in 2012.

Photo Courtesy of Nicole Cameron

what had to happen, but oh how I prayed that Casey would drift off to sleep at home in my arms. Casey's story with me has been chronicled in *Rescuing Used Coonhounds*.

I spent my last night with Casey lying on the couch, stroking him in his dog bed. All night. I told him how much I loved him, the story of rescuing him, and how much I loved him and his beautiful songs. I repeated all of that as his veterinarian administered the dreaded medicine that would take my Casey away from me. I've had to have several dogs put to sleep. It is never easy. But my Treeing Walker Coonhound was different. I can't explain it. Perhaps it was because Casey had had such a hard and abusive life before we rescued each other. It simply wasn't fair that I wouldn't get to celebrate his 15th birthday. Casey was about eight years old. He was middle-aged. So am I.

The attachment/bonding/relationship you will have with your Treeing Walker Coonhound can only be experienced. You can read about it but until you live it, I don't think you will fully understand how these very special coonhounds wind their way into our lives. And hearts.

Photo Courtesy of Carly Ferguson

The Euthanasia Process

Although saying good-bye to your coonhound will never ever be easy, the euthanasia process in and of itself is relatively painless. No one wants their pets to suffer.

If you know that your Treeing Walker Coonhound is ill and will not recover, you can contact your veterinarian to be "on standby" when you need his or her services. Many veterinarians will come to your house so your coonhound can be at home in a familiar and loving environment. Consult with your veterinarian and see if this is an option.

Should you have to take your coonhound to your veterinarian's office, ensure that you will have privacy. It usually isn't a problem and the veterinarian knows what you will experience. The examination rooms at my veterinarian's office have windows, but there is a special examination room with a small sofa, chairs and a nice rug. The window shade is pulled down for privacy. Unless it is an emergency, you might opt for an early morning or late afternoon appointment, when there is less noise and hustle and bustle, to bring your coonhound friend to the vet.

Many veterinarians are now opting to give intravenous sedatives to animals before they are euthanized. When the needle is inserted, the veterinarian will leave a port through which the sedative and the euthanasia medicine will be injected. This is for the comfort of your coonhound, so he won't have to be stuck with a needle multiple times.

Once the sedative is administered, your veterinarian will give you time to tell your beloved coonhound good-bye. The sedative helps to calm your hound, in the event that he is nervous or hurting. It relaxes him so he can listen to you tell him how much you love him.

My final moments with Casey were spent kissing him and telling him the story of when we met, how I enjoyed his beautiful songs, thanking him for his songs and coming into my life, and how very, very much I loved him and how I would miss him. Tell your coonhound your stories. Let him see you. Stroke him and tell him over and over again how much you love him.

The euthanasia medicine is designed to completely relax the muscles and prevent nerve transmission. It is painless and quiet. As your veterinarian administers the solution, continue to tell your coonhound how much he is loved. Within 15 seconds, he may take a deep breath or two, and then he will become motionless. Your veterinarian will check for a heartbeat. Continue to tell your coonhound how much he is loved, even after the veterinarian doesn't detect a heartbeat.

It will be extremely difficult to stay with your hound during this process. I understand. But my face and my voice were the last things I wanted Casey to see and hear and take with him. Your coonhound will appreciate seeing you one last time and hearing your voice. I don't think you will ever regret being with your beloved Treeing Walker Coonhound in the final moments of his life on this earth. You may second-guess your decision, over and over again, but being with him until the very end is something that is priceless. I have often told myself that maybe I should have waited. Done this. Done that. Deep down I know I was doing the right thing. My veterinarian told me that, too. But my heart still broke into a million pieces. It is not easy. But it is not easy watching our pets suffer, either. That's part of our job. We are responsible for the well-being and safety and comfort of our coonhounds. No matter how difficult it can be.

The Final Resting Place

You will need to decide if you want to bury your best friend or have him cremated. If you know that you are never moving and have the space, you might think of burying your beloved coonhound, selecting a quiet and peaceful spot that is just perfect for him, perhaps even wrapping him in his favorite blanket or a shirt of yours and adding a toy or bone. You might have a grave marker or memorial plaque made for your coonhound friend. Maybe you decide to plant a tree or flowers over his grave. Make this as personal as possible. Your grief is personal. Remember that. Anything you do is okay.

Should you decide to have your buddy cremated, you have more options. I had Casey, and several other beloved dogs, cremated. My veterinarian offers cremation services through a cremation company, as many veterinarians do. I have been able to select the urn and pay for the services at the time of saying good-bye to my pets. (I have also had to call the cremation company in the past and that is a very difficult thing to do.) It helps ease the pain somewhat with the veterinary receptionist making the arrangements for you. And unless you are going to bury your coonhound in a special place, his body will remain at the veterinarian's office for the cremation company to pick up. Picking up his remains from the veterinarian was difficult and just when I didn't think I could cry anymore, I discovered that I could.

I put the wooden box with paw prints that contained Casey's remains in a drawer in my nightstand. I had a plaster mold of his paw print made, too. His collar is on my nightstand and I plan to get a shadowbox for it.

On the third anniversary of finding Casey and bringing him home, I opened the box and sprinkled some of his remains around my backyard.

Casey was a guardian at the gates, so I made sure that he will always be there guarding me. He had a favorite place behind the butterfly bush where he looked into the trees for raccoons. He actually knew one was there one time and wouldn't leave his post. I found it the next day as it had apparently fallen out of the tree or was old and sick. Regardless, Casey knew it was there. I put some of his remains there, so he could always look for raccoons. I put the box and the rest of his remains back in my nightstand.

Never Forget Your Best Friend

I didn't have Casey nearly long enough, but I don't think having him the rest of my life would be long enough. I feel exactly the same way about Bowie.

Your Treeing Walker Coonhound will give you the best that he has to give. He will be your friend and companion as long as he can. Honor him. Hang up photos of him. Write down stories about him. Remember him every day. I can't begin to tell you how special these dogs are, although I have tried to in this book. Once you get your very own Treeing Walker Coonhound, you will discover this firsthand. And I don't think that you will ever be the same again.

REFERENCES

"A Guide to Hunting Raccoons," raccoonhunting.com

"Artificial Fragrances: These Are Poison To Your Dog," Dr. Edward Bassingthwaighte

The Complete Dog Breed Book, Dorling Kindersley, DK Publishing, 2012

Dogs: The Ultimate Care Guide, Lowell Ackerman, D.V.M., Ph.D., Weldon Owen, Inc., St. Martin's Press, 1998

Inside of a Dog: What Dogs See, Smell, and Know, Alexandra Horowitz, Simon & Schuster, Inc., 2009

Lucky Dog Lessons, Brandon McMillan, Animal Expert LLC, HarperCollins Publishers, 2016

The Mini-Atlas of Dog Breeds, Andrew De Prisco and James B. Johnson, T.F.H. Publications, 1990

https://www.akccoonhounds.org

https://www.akc.org/dog-breeds/treeing-walker-coonhound/

https://www.akc.org/expert-advice/health/bloat-in-dogs

https://www.akc.org/expert-advice/health/cushings-disease-in-dogs/

https://www.akc.org/expert-advice/health/how-to-get-rid-of-fleas/

https://www.akc.org/expert-advice/health/puppy-shots-complete-guide/

https://www.akc.org/expert-advice/health/the-dog-flu-symptoms-you-need-to-know/

https://www.akc.org/expert-advice/health/thyroid-disease-in-dogs

https://www.akc.org/expert-advice/health/what-to-do-if-your-dog-ate-chocolate/

https://www.akc.org/expert-advice/home-living/household-hazards-poisons-for-dogs/

https://www.akc.org/expert-advice/lifestyle/how-do-dog-microchips-work/

https://www.akc.org/sports/field-events-hounds/coonhounds/

https://www.appalachianhistory.net/2018/11/maupins-walkers-and-tennessee-lead.html

https://www.carecredit.com/vetmed/article/10-things-dogs-ears/

https://www.cesarsway.com/through-a-dogs-eyes/

https://www.diamondpet.com/blog/health/sensitive-skin/dogs-skin-coat-layer/

https://www.dog.com/content/dog-health/dog-eye-facts/

https://www.dogbreedsfaq.com/dog-questions/dog-pros-and-cons/dog-jowls/

https://www.dogbreedinfo.com/treeingwalkercoonhound.htm

https://www.doghealth.com/health/ears/1918-hearing-in-dogs

https://www.dog-health-guide.org/toxic-to-dogs.html

https://www.dummies.com/pets/dogs/understanding-a-dogs-sense-of-smell/

https://www.en.wikipedia.org/wiki/Tick

https://fasdawg.tripod.com/history.html, Walkerhound.com, C.J. Prouty, 1907

https://www.greenfieldpuppies.com "7 Signs You Should Get Your Dog's Thyroid Checked

https://www.heartwormsociety.org/heartworms-in-dogs

https://www.hmdb.org/m.asp?m=68327

https://www.iheartdogs.com/8-fun-facts-about-your-dogs-ears/

https://www.morningchores.com/plants-poisonous-to-dogs/

https://www.pbs.org/wgbh/nova/article/dogs-sense-of-smell/

https://www.petfinder.com/pet-adoption/dog-adoption/why-do-bloodhounds-have-long-ears/

https://www.petfriendlyhouse.com/facts-about-dog-hearing/

https://www.petful.com/pet-health/ectropion-in-dogs-treatment/

https://www.petsdoc.org/through-the-eyes-of-your-dog/

https://www.petmd.com/dog/behavior/5-dog-nose-facts-you-probably-didn't-know

https://www.petmd.com/dog/care/evr_dg_euthanasia_what_to_expect

https://www.petmd.com/dog/care/how-many-teeth-do-dogs-have-and-can-they-lose-them

https://www.petmd.com/dog/care/puppy-teeth-everything-you-need-to-know

https://www.petmd.com/dog/chocolate-toxicity

https://www.petmd.com/dog/slideshows/6-fascinating-facts-about-your-dogs-eyes#slide-4

https://www.pets.webmd.com/dogs/how-to-calculate-your-dogs-age
https://www.scienceabc.com/nature/animals/why-dogs-sense-of-smell-is-so-good.html

https://www.thesprucepets.com/dog-sense-of-smell-4776425

https://www.thesprucepets.com/puppy-teething-2804965

https://www.thesprucepets.com/toxic-foods-and-your-dog-1117869

https://www.thesprucepets.com/treating-eyelid-entropion-in-dogs-508574

https://www.ukcdogs.com/coonhound-about

https://www.vcahospitals.com/know-your-pet/cherry-eye-in-dogs

https://www.vcahospitals.com/know-your-pet/testing-for-heartworm-disease-in-dogs

https://www.vetanswers.com.au

https://www.vetmed.illinois.edu/pet_column/hope-for-heartworm-positive-dogs/

https://www.vetstreet.com/dogs/treeing-walker-coonhound

https://www.wikihow.com/Identify-mange-on-dogs

https://www.yourpurebredpuppy.com/health/coonhounds.html

Made in the USA
Monee, IL
13 April 2022

94656612R00109